Grammar
Plus
Writing

②

저자 약력

전지원   미국 오리건 주립대 Linguistics 석사
(현) 한국 외국어대학교 외국어연수 평가원 영어 전임 강사
〈내공 중학 영작문〉(다락원), 〈Grammar Mate〉(다락원),
〈Grammar's Cool〉(YBM), 〈빠르게 잡는 영문법〉(천재교육) 등 다수의 교재 공저

박혜영   미국 하와이 주립대 Second Language Studies 석사
(현) 한국 외국어대학교 외국어연수 평가원 영어 전임 강사
〈내공 중학 영작문〉(다락원), 〈Grammar Mate〉(다락원),
〈Grammar's Cool〉(YBM), 〈빠르게 잡는 영문법〉(천재교육) 등 다수의 교재 공저

Grammar +Plus Writing ❷

지은이 전지원, 박혜영

펴낸이 정규도
펴낸곳 (주)다락원

개정판 1쇄 발행 2023년 12월 11일
개정판 3쇄 발행 2024년 12월 5일

편집 서정아, 안혜원, 신채영
디자인 구수정, 포레스트
삽화 강정연
영문 감수 Michael A. Putlack

다락원 경기도 파주시 문발로 211
내용문의 (02)736-2031 내선 503
구입문의 (02)736-2031 내선 250~252

Fax (02)732-2037
출판등록 1977년 9월 16일 제 406-2008-000007호

ISBN 978-89-277-8065-6 54740
       978-89-277-8063-2 54740(set)

http://www.darakwon.co.kr
다락원 홈페이지를 방문하시면 상세한 출판정보와 함께
동영상강좌, MP3 자료 등 다양한 어학 정보를 얻으실 수 있습니다.

Grammar
Plus
Writing

2

STRUCTURES | 구성과 특징

> ### Grammar Plus Writing 시리즈는
> - 중등 필수 영문법을 쉽고 빠르게 습득할 수 있습니다.
> - 학습한 문법 요소를 영작과 연계하여 문법 지식과 영작 능력을 동시에 향상시킬 수 있습니다.
> - 최신 기출 유형과 고난도 문제로 내신 및 서술형 시험에 효과적으로 대비할 수 있습니다.

GRAMMAR FOCUS

내신뿐 아니라 영작을 할 때 꼭 필요한 중등 필수 영문법을 선별하여 쉽고 간결하게 제시했습니다.
문법 학습 후에는 단계별 Exercise를 통해 학습한 내용을 체계적으로 점검할 수 있습니다.

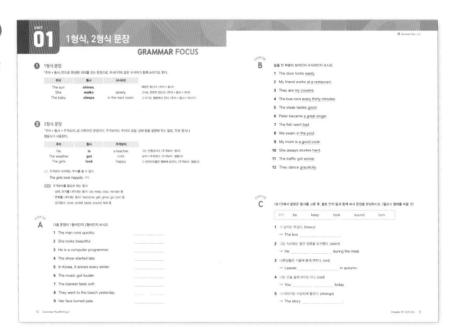

WRITING FOCUS

학습한 문법 요소를 활용하여 영작 훈련을 하는 코너입니다. 영작에 대한 자신감을 키우고 학교 시험에 자주 나오는 문제 유형(배열 영작, 문장 완성, 문장 전환, 오류 수정 등)을 통해 서술형 시험에 효과적으로 대비할 수 있습니다.

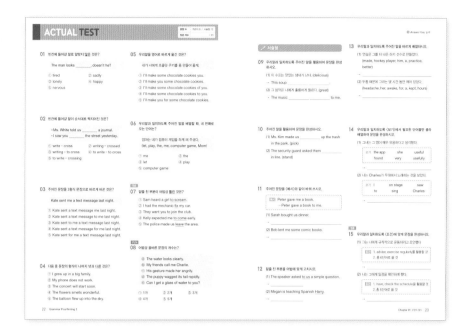

ACTUAL TEST

챕터 학습이 끝난 후, 내신 유형의 문제를 풀어보며 학습한 내용을 정리합니다. 최신 빈출 유형과 고난도 유형을 수록했으며, 50% 이상이 서술형 문제로 구성되어 어려워진 내신 시험에 철저히 대비할 수 있습니다.

WORKBOOK

별책으로 제공되는 워크북에서는 각 Unit의 문법사항을 Worksheet 형태로 제공하여 학습한 내용을 빠르게 복습하고 실력을 점검할 수 있습니다.

온라인 부가자료 | www.darakwon.co.kr

다락원 홈페이지에서 무료로 부가자료를 다운로드하거나 웹에서 이용하실 수 있습니다.

CONTENTS | 목차

Chapter 01

문장의 형식

GRAMMAR FOCUS

1 **1형식 문장**

「주어 + 동사」만으로 완성된 의미를 갖는 문장으로, 부사(구)와 같은 수식어가 함께 쓰이기도 한다.

주어	동사	(수식어)
The sun	**shines**.	
She	**walks**	slowly.
The baby	**sleeps**	in the next room.

태양은 빛난다. 〈주어 + 동사〉
그녀는 천천히 걷는다. 〈주어 + 동사 + 부사〉
그 아기는 옆방에서 잔다. 〈주어 + 동사 + 부사구〉

2 **2형식 문장**

「주어 + 동사 + 주격보어」로 이루어진 문장이다. 주격보어는 주어의 성질, 상태 등을 설명해 주는 말로, 주로 명사나 형용사가 사용된다.

주어	동사	주격보어
He	**is**	a teacher.
The weather	**got**	cold.
The girls	**look**	happy.

그는 선생님이다. 〈주격보어: 명사〉
날씨가 추워졌다. 〈주격보어: 형용사〉
그 여자아이들은 행복해 보인다. 〈주격보어: 형용사〉

cf. 주격보어 자리에는 부사를 쓸 수 없다.

The girls look *happily*. (×)

plus 주격보어를 필요로 하는 동사
  • 상태, 유지를 나타내는 동사: be, keep, stay, remain 등
  • 변화를 나타내는 동사: become, get, grow, go, turn 등
  • 감각동사: look, smell, taste, sound, feel 등

다음 문장이 1형식인지 2형식인지 쓰시오.

1 The man runs quickly. _____

2 She looks beautiful. _____

3 He is a computer programmer. _____

4 The show started late. _____

5 In Korea, it snows every winter. _____

6 The music got louder. _____

7 The blanket feels soft. _____

8 They went to the beach yesterday. _____

9 Her face turned pale. _____

EXERCISE B

밑줄 친 부분이 보어인지 수식어인지 쓰시오.

1 The door locks <u>easily</u>.

2 My friend works <u>at a restaurant</u>.

3 They are <u>my cousins</u>.

4 The bus runs <u>every thirty minutes</u>.

5 The steak tastes <u>good</u>.

6 Peter became <u>a great singer</u>.

7 The fish went <u>bad</u>.

8 We swam <u>in the pool</u>.

9 My mom is <u>a good cook</u>.

10 She always studies <u>hard</u>.

11 The traffic got <u>worse</u>.

12 They dance <u>gracefully</u>.

EXERCISE C

〈보기〉에서 알맞은 동사를 고른 후, 괄호 안의 말과 함께 써서 문장을 완성하시오. (필요시 형태를 바꿀 것)

보기	be	keep	look	sound	turn

1 그 상자는 무겁다. (heavy)

　→ The box _____ _____.

2 그는 식사하는 동안 침묵을 유지했다. (silent)

　→ He _____ _____ during the meal.

3 나뭇잎들은 가을에 붉게 변한다. (red)

　→ Leaves _____ _____ in autumn.

4 너는 오늘 슬퍼 보이는구나. (sad)

　→ You _____ _____ today.

5 그 이야기는 이상하게 들린다. (strange)

　→ The story _____ _____.

WRITING FOCUS

A 배열 영작   우리말과 일치하도록 괄호 안의 말을 바르게 배열하시오.

1 내 여동생은 노래를 잘한다. (my, sings, well, sister)

➡ _____

2 태양은 동쪽에서 뜬다. (the, in, the, east, sun, rises)

➡ _____

3 오늘은 나의 생일이다. (birthday, is, my, today)

➡ _____

4 그 판매원은 우리에게 친절했다. (the, to, was, kind, us, salesclerk)

➡ _____

5 Rick은 작년에 중학생이 되었다. (last year, a, became, middle school student, Rick)

➡ _____

6 이 곡은 지루하게 들린다. (boring, this, sounds, song)

➡ _____

B 빈칸 완성   우리말과 일치하도록 괄호 안의 말을 이용하여 빈칸에 알맞은 말을 쓰시오.

1 나의 조부모님은 시골에 사신다. (grandparents, live)

➡ _____ _____ _____ in the country.

2 그 수업은 9시에 시작한다. (class, start)

➡ _____ _____ _____ at nine.

3 한국에서는 여름에 비가 많이 온다. (it, rain)

➡ In Korea, _____ _____ a lot in summer.

4 그의 방은 매우 깨끗하다. (very clean)

➡ His room _____ _____ _____.

5 그 수프는 짠맛이 난다. (taste, salty)

➡ The soup _____ _____.

6 이 소파는 편안하게 느껴진다. (feel, comfortable)

➡ This sofa _____ _____.

C 문장 완성　　우리말과 일치하도록 괄호 안의 말을 이용하여 문장을 완성하시오.

1 그는 매우 빨리 달린다. (run, very fast)

→ _____

2 나는 매일 아침 조깅을 한다. (jog, every morning)

→ _____

3 그것은 내 잘못이야. (it, fault)

→ _____

4 그의 신곡은 인기를 얻었다. (new song, become, popular)

→ _____

5 그 물은 차갑게 느껴진다. (water, feel, cold)

→ _____

6 그 과일은 달콤한 향기가 난다. (fruit, smell, sweet)

→ _____

D 오류 수정　　어법상 틀린 부분을 바르게 고쳐 문장을 다시 쓰시오.

1 She smiles happy. (그녀는 행복하게 웃는다.)

→ _____

2 Ted swims very good. (Ted는 수영을 매우 잘한다.)

→ _____

3 October 3 is tomorrow. (내일은 10월 3일이다.)

→ _____

4 The suitcase is heavily. (그 여행 가방은 무겁다.)

→ _____

5 The music sounds beautifully. (그 음악은 아름답게 들린다.)

→ _____

6 The dog became health again. (그 개는 다시 건강해졌다.)

→ _____

UNIT 02 3형식, 4형식 문장

GRAMMAR FOCUS

① 3형식 문장

「주어 + 동사 + 목적어」로 이루어진 문장이다. 목적어 자리에는 명사, 대명사, to부정사(구), 동명사(구), 명사절이 올 수 있다.

주어	동사	목적어	
Bob	**drives**	a bus.	Bob은 버스를 운전한다. 〈목적어: 명사〉
I	**want**	to go home.	나는 집에 가기를 원한다. 〈목적어: to부정사구〉
She	**enjoys**	traveling alone.	그녀는 혼자 여행하는 것을 즐긴다. 〈목적어: 동명사구〉

② 4형식 문장

(1) 「주어 + 동사 + 간접목적어(…에게) + 직접목적어(~을)」로 이루어진 문장이다. 4형식 문장에는 '~(해) 주다'라는 의미의 수여동사가 쓰인다.

주어	수여동사	간접목적어	직접목적어	
I	**gave**	my friend	a gift.	나는 내 친구에게 선물 하나를 주었다.
My mom	**made**	me	breakfast.	엄마는 나에게 아침을 만들어 주셨다.
We	**asked**	him	a question.	우리는 그에게 질문 하나를 했다.

(2) 4형식 문장은 「주어 + 동사 + 직접목적어 + 전치사 + 간접목적어」 형태의 3형식 문장으로 바꿔 쓸 수 있다.

주어	수여동사	직접목적어	전치사	간접목적어
I	**gave**	a gift	**to**	my friend.
My mom	**made**	breakfast	**for**	me.
We	**asked**	a question	**of**	him.

plus 간접목적어 앞에 쓰는 전치사
- to를 쓰는 동사: give, teach, send, bring, show, tell, write, lend 등
- for를 쓰는 동사: make, cook, buy, get, find 등
- of를 쓰는 동사: ask

EXERCISE A

다음 문장이 3형식인지 4형식인지 쓰시오.

1 I like fruits and vegetables. _____

2 He showed me the picture. _____

3 My friend lent her tent to me. _____

4 Jimmy told me the truth. _____

5 I will send you an email. _____

6 She bought a gift for her husband. _____

EXERCISE
B

두 문장의 의미가 같도록 빈칸에 to, for, of 중 알맞은 것을 쓰시오.

1 I bought my mom a nice necklace.

→ I bought a nice necklace _____ my mom.

2 Mr. Stevens taught us English for two years.

→ Mr. Stevens taught English _____ us for two years.

3 She didn't ask me anything.

→ She didn't ask anything _____ me.

4 I will bring you a warm blanket.

→ I will bring a warm blanket _____ you.

5 My grandmother made me this sweater.

→ My grandmother made this sweater _____ me.

6 The old man didn't tell us the story.

→ The old man didn't tell the story _____ us.

EXERCISE
C

밑줄 친 부분을 바르게 고쳐 문장을 다시 쓰시오.

1 He showed <u>to us</u> some photos.

→ _____

2 She bought a new pair of shoes <u>to him</u>.

→ _____

3 They asked <u>of me</u> a difficult question.

→ _____

4 My friend sent a postcard <u>for me</u>.

→ _____

5 I didn't write any letters <u>him</u>.

→ _____

6 The neighbor made some cookies <u>to us</u>.

→ _____

WRITING FOCUS

A 배열 영작   우리말과 일치하도록 괄호 안의 말을 바르게 배열하시오.

1 Jack과 Mary는 생선을 좋아한다. (like, fish, Jack and Mary)

→ _____

2 나는 해양 생물에 관한 책 한 권을 읽었다. (read, I, about sea life, a book)

→ _____

3 뉴욕에 있는 내 친구는 나에게 선물 하나를 보냈다. (my friend in New York, sent, a gift, me)

→ _____

4 그 소년은 나에게 꽃을 몇 송이 가져다 주었다. (me, the boy, some flowers, brought)

→ _____

5 그녀는 우리에게 국사를 가르친다. (to, Korean history, she, teaches, us)

→ _____

6 Sam은 그의 친구에게 멋진 셔츠를 사 주었다. (bought, for, Sam, his friend, a nice shirt)

→ _____

B 빈칸 완성   우리말과 일치하도록 괄호 안의 말을 이용하여 빈칸에 알맞은 말을 쓰시오.

1 나는 하루 종일 아무것도 먹지 않았다. (eat, anything)

→ I didn't _____ _____ all day.

2 나의 아버지는 매일 아침 신문을 읽으신다. (read, the newspaper)

→ My father _____ _____ _____ every morning.

3 Mike는 우리에게 그 소식을 말해 주었다. (the news)

→ Mike told _____ _____ _____.

4 많은 팬들이 그에게 선물을 보냈다. (gifts)

→ A lot of fans sent _____ _____.

5 나는 내 여동생에게 케이크를 만들어 주었다. (a cake)

→ I made _____ _____ _____ my sister.

6 Wilson 선생님은 우리에게 과학을 가르치신다. (science)

→ Mr. Wilson teaches _____ _____ _____.

C 문장 완성   우리말과 일치하도록 괄호 안의 말을 이용하여 문장을 완성하시오.

1 Sally는 매일 첼로를 연주한다. (play, the cello)

→ _____ every day.

2 나는 길에서 내 중학교 친구를 만났다. (meet, middle school friend)

→ _____ on the street.

3 그는 나에게 자신의 숙제를 보여 주었다. (show)

→ _____ his homework.

4 나는 Susan에게 생일 카드를 만들어 주었다. (make)

→ _____ a birthday card.

5 Steve는 우리에게 약간의 간식을 주었다. (give, some snacks)

→ _____ us.

6 Cindy는 그녀의 친구들에게 저녁을 요리해 주었다. (cook, dinner)

→ _____ her friends.

D 오류 수정   밑줄 친 부분을 바르게 고쳐 문장을 다시 쓰시오.

1 Did you watch <u>yesterday the movie</u>?

→ _____

2 Mary lent her tablet PC <u>for me</u>.

→ _____

3 Many girls sent letters <u>the singer</u>.

→ _____

4 We asked a lot of questions <u>to the new teacher</u>.

→ _____

5 My parents give <u>to me</u> a lot of love.

→ _____

6 He didn't tell <u>the truth them</u>.

→ _____

① 5형식 문장

「주어 + 동사 + 목적어 + 목적격보어」로 이루어진 문장이다. 목적격보어는 목적어의 성질, 상태 등을 설명해 주는 말로, 명사(구), 형용사(구), to부정사(구) 등이 사용된다.

주어	동사	목적어	목적격보어	
We	**call**	him	Andy.	우리는 그를 Andy라고 부른다. 〈목적격보어: 명사〉
The news	**made**	us	sad.	그 소식은 우리를 슬프게 만들었다. 〈목적격보어: 형용사〉
She	**told**	me	to rest.	그녀는 나에게 쉬라고 말했다. 〈목적격보어: to부정사〉

plus 동사에 따른 목적격보어의 종류
- 명사: call, name, make, elect 등
- 형용사: make, keep, leave, find 등
- to부정사: want, tell, ask, expect, advise, allow 등

② 사역동사

'~가 …하게 하다 / 시키다'의 의미를 갖는 사역동사 make, have, let은 목적격보어로 동사원형이 온다.

주어	동사	목적어	목적격보어	
My mom	**made**	us	**clean** the room.	엄마는 우리에게 방을 청소하도록 시키셨다.
I	**had**	him	**fix** the car.	나는 그에게 차를 고치게 했다.
Tom	**let**	me	**ride** his bicycle.	Tom은 내가 그의 자전거를 타게 해 주었다.

③ 지각동사

'~가 …하는 것을 보다 / 듣다 / 느끼다 / 냄새를 맡다'의 의미를 갖는 지각동사 see, hear, feel, smell 등은 목적격보어로 동사원형이 온다.

주어	동사	목적어	목적격보어	
She	**saw**	the kids	**play** around.	그녀는 아이들이 뛰어노는 것을 보았다.
I	**felt**	the ground	**shake**.	나는 땅이 흔들리는 것을 느꼈다.

cf. 동작이 진행 중임을 강조할 때는 지각동사의 목적격보어로 현재분사를 쓴다.

She **saw** the kids **playing** around. 그녀는 아이들이 뛰어놀고 있는 것을 보았다.

A

다음 문장에서 목적어에는 ○, 목적격보어에는 밑줄로 표시하시오.

1 We usually call him Mr. Robinson.

2 He kept the bedroom door open.

3 I want you to read that book.

4 My friend let me use his computer.

5 Sarah heard the man sing a beautiful song.

EXERCISE B

괄호 안에서 알맞은 것을 고르시오.

1 We call him (Captain, to Captain).

2 I found the chair (comfortable, comfortably).

3 My parents want me (to be, being) a professor.

4 I felt something (touch, to touch) my back.

5 My doctor advised me (get, to get) some rest.

6 I heard someone (call, called) my name.

7 He didn't let me (use, to use) his phone.

8 Does your mom allow you (go, to go) out at night?

9 The news about Eric made us (happy, happily).

10 Can you see her (stands, standing) over there?

11 We expect him (to pass, passing) the exam.

12 She made her son (practice, to practice) the piano.

EXERCISE C

우리말과 일치하도록 〈보기〉에서 알맞은 말을 골라 문장을 완성하시오. (필요시 형태를 바꿀 것)

보기	cut	hero	sit	angry	dance

1 그들은 나를 영웅이라고 불렀다.

→ They called me a(n) _____.

2 그 소년의 변명은 우리를 화나게 했다.

→ The boy's excuses made us _____.

3 그 버스 운전사는 승객들에게 앉아 달라고 요청했다.

→ The bus driver asked the passengers _____ down.

4 나는 미용사에게 내 머리를 자르게 했다.

→ I had the hairdresser _____ my hair.

5 너는 Jerry가 무대에서 춤추는 것을 보았니?

→ Did you see Jerry _____ on stage?

WRITING FOCUS

A 배열 영작   우리말과 일치하도록 괄호 안의 말을 바르게 배열하시오.

1 그들은 나를 천사라고 불렀다. (angel, they, called, an, me)

→ _____

2 그 소식은 우리를 행복하게 만들었다. (the, us, happy, made, news)

→ _____

3 우리는 Sophia를 반장으로 선출했다. (Sophia, we, class president, elected)

→ _____

4 엄마는 나에게 컴퓨터를 끄도록 시키셨다. (my mom, me, computer, made, the, turn off)

→ _____

5 나는 그 도둑이 달아나는 것을 보았다. (thief, saw, I, the, running away)

→ _____

6 Janet은 내가 그녀의 가방을 들어 주기를 원했다. (Janet, her, wanted, carry, me, to, bag)

→ _____

B 빈칸 완성   우리말과 일치하도록 괄호 안의 말을 이용하여 빈칸에 알맞은 말을 쓰시오.

1 나는 그녀의 목소리가 이상하다고 생각했다. (find, strange)

→ I _____ her voice _____.

2 아빠는 내 남동생을 Anthony라고 이름 지으셨다. (name, my brother)

→ Dad _____ _____ _____ _____.

3 Mary는 내가 그녀의 휴대폰을 쓰게 해 주었다. (let, use)

→ Mary _____ _____ _____ her cellphone.

4 나는 그들이 해변에서 노는 것을 보았다. (see, play)

→ I _____ _____ _____ at the beach.

5 우리는 Brian이 그의 친구들과 이야기하는 것을 들었다. (hear, talk)

→ We _____ _____ _____ with his friends.

6 그 남자는 나에게 한 번 더 설명해 달라고 부탁했다. (ask, explain)

→ The man _____ _____ _____ _____ one more time.

C 문장 완성 우리말과 일치하도록 괄호 안의 말을 이용하여 문장을 완성하시오.

1 우리는 그를 천재라고 불렀다. (call, a genius)

→ We _____ .

2 Joseph은 그 책이 지루하다고 생각했다. (find, book, boring)

→ Joseph _____ .

3 선생님은 Mark에게 조용히 하라고 말씀하셨다. (tell, quiet)

→ The teacher _____ .

4 엄마는 나에게 설거지를 하도록 시키셨다. (make, do the dishes)

→ My mom _____ .

5 우리는 여러분이 우리 동아리에 가입하기를 기대해요. (expect, join our club)

→ We _____ .

6 Cindy는 누군가가 자신의 어깨를 만지는 것을 느꼈다. (feel, someone, touch her shoulder)

→ Cindy _____ .

D 오류 수정 어법상 <u>틀린</u> 부분을 바르게 고쳐 문장을 다시 쓰시오.

1 These earmuffs will keep you warmly. (이 귀마개는 너를 따뜻하게 해 줄 것이다.)

→ _____

2 I told her close the door. (나는 그녀에게 문을 닫으라고 말했다.)

→ _____

3 Did you hear the baby to cry? (당신은 그 아기가 우는 것을 들었습니까?)

→ _____

4 My mom doesn't let me skipping breakfast. (엄마는 내가 아침을 식사를 거르지 못하게 하신다.)

→ _____

5 The comedy movie made us laughed. (그 코미디 영화는 우리를 웃게 했다.)

→ _____

6 The coach advised Jack practicing more. (그 코치는 Jack에게 더 연습하라고 조언했다.)

→ _____

01 빈칸에 들어갈 말로 알맞지 <u>않은</u> 것은?

> The man looks _____, doesn't he?

① tired   ② sadly
③ lonely   ④ happy
⑤ nervous

02 빈칸에 들어갈 말이 순서대로 짝지어진 것은?

> • Ms. White told us _____ a journal.
> • I saw you _____ the street yesterday.

① write – cross   ② writing – crossed
③ writing – to cross   ④ to write – to cross
⑤ to write – crossing

03 주어진 문장을 3형식 문장으로 바르게 바꾼 것은?

> Kate sent me a text message last night.

① Kate sent a text message me last night.
② Kate sent a text message to me last night.
③ Kate sent to me a text message last night.
④ Kate sent a text message for me last night.
⑤ Kate sent for me a text message last night.

04 다음 중 문장의 형식이 나머지 넷과 <u>다른</u> 것은?

① I grew up in a big family.
② My phone does not work.
③ The concert will start soon.
④ The flowers smells wonderful.
⑤ The balloon flew up into the sky.

05 우리말을 영어로 바르게 옮긴 것은?

> 내가 너에게 초콜릿 쿠키를 좀 만들어 줄게.

① I'll make some chocolate cookies you.
② I'll make you some chocolate cookies.
③ I'll make some chocolate cookies of you.
④ I'll make some chocolate cookies to you.
⑤ I'll make you for some chocolate cookies.

06 우리말과 일치하도록 주어진 말을 배열할 때, 네 번째로 오는 단어는?

> 엄마는 내가 컴퓨터 게임을 하게 해 주셨다.
> (let, play, the, me, computer game, Mom)

① me   ② the
③ let   ④ play
⑤ computer game

빈출
07 밑줄 친 부분이 어법상 <u>틀린</u> 것은?

① Sam heard a girl <u>to scream</u>.
② I had the mechanic <u>fix</u> my car.
③ They want you <u>to join</u> the club.
④ Kelly expected me <u>to come</u> early.
⑤ The police made us <u>leave</u> the area.

고난도
08 어법상 올바른 문장의 개수는?

ⓐ The water looks clearly.
ⓑ My friends call me Charlie.
ⓒ His gesture made her angrily.
ⓓ The puppy wagged its tail rapidly.
ⓔ Can I get a glass of water to you?

① 1개   ② 2개   ③ 3개
④ 4개   ⑤ 5개

✏️ **서술형**

09 우리말과 일치하도록 주어진 말을 활용하여 문장을 완성하시오.

(1) 이 수프는 맛있는 냄새가 난다. (delicious)

→ This soup _____ _____ .

(2) 그 음악은 나에게 훌륭하게 들린다. (great)

→ The music _____ _____ to me.

10 주어진 말을 활용하여 문장을 완성하시오.

(1) Ms. Kim made us _____ up the trash in the park. (pick)

(2) The security guard asked them _____ in line. (stand)

11 주어진 문장을 〈예시〉와 같이 바꿔 쓰시오.

> 예시 Peter gave me a book.
> → Peter gave a book to me.

(1) Sarah bought us dinner.

→ _____

(2) Bob lent me some comic books.

→ _____

12 밑줄 친 부분을 어법에 맞게 고치시오.

(1) The speaker asked to us a simple question.

→ _____

(2) Megan is teaching Spanish Harry.

→ _____

13 우리말과 일치하도록 주어진 말을 바르게 배열하시오.

(1) 연습은 그를 더 나은 하키 선수로 만들었다.

(made, hockey player, him, a, practice, better)

→ _____

(2) 두통 때문에 그녀는 몇 시간 동안 깨어 있었다.

(headache, her, awake, for, a, kept, hours)

→ _____

14 우리말과 일치하도록 〈보기〉에서 필요한 단어들만 골라 배열하여 문장을 완성하시오.

(1) 그녀는 그 앱이 매우 유용하다고 생각했다.

보기	the app	she	useful
	found	very	usefully

→ _____

(2) 나는 Charles가 무대에서 노래하는 것을 보았다.

보기	I	on stage	saw
	to	sing	Charles

→ _____

빈출
15 우리말과 일치하도록 〈조건〉에 맞게 문장을 완성하시오.

(1) 그는 나에게 규칙적으로 운동하라고 조언했다

> 조건 1. advise, exercise regularly를 활용할 것
> 2. 총 6단어로 쓸 것

→ _____

(2) 나는 그에게 일정을 확인하게 했다.

> 조건 1. have, check the schedule을 활용할 것
> 2. 총 6단어로 쓸 것

→ _____

16 그림을 보고, 각 상자에서 필요한 말을 하나씩 골라 알맞은 형태로 써서 문장을 완성하시오.

(1)  (2)

| smell sound | loud good |

(1) The music _____ _____.

(2) This coffee _____ _____.

17 다음은 태풍을 겪은 사람들의 진술이다. 각 사람의 진술을 활용하여 주어진 문장을 완성하시오.

Who	What
John	The wind got stronger.
Kate	The windows rattled loudly.
Mike	Some trees fell down.

(1) John felt _____.

(2) Kate heard _____.

(3) Mike saw _____.

18 어법상 틀린 문장 2개를 골라 기호를 쓰고, 틀린 부분을 바르게 고치시오.

ⓐ My father goes to work by bus.
ⓑ The new movie looks interestingly.
ⓒ Billy brought his goldfish to school.
ⓓ My mom cooked me seaweed soup on my birthday.
ⓔ My parents let me to sleep over at my friend's house.

( ) _____ → _____

( ) _____ → _____

[19-20] 대화를 읽고, 물음에 답하시오.

A: You ⓐlook worried. What happened?
B: I have some science homework. It's too difficult.
A: When is the deadline?
B: 선생님께서 우리에게 월요일까지 숙제를 제출하라고 말씀하셨어. I ⓑneed some help.
A: I ⓒsaw Sam studied in the library. Why don't you ⓓask him to help you? He is good at science.
B: That's a great idea. Thank you.

고난도
19 어법상 틀린 것을 찾아 기호를 쓰고 바르게 고치시오.

( ) → _____

20 밑줄 친 우리말과 일치하도록 〈조건〉에 맞게 문장을 완성하시오.

조건 tell, hand in, our homework를 활용할 것

→ The teacher _____

_____ by Monday.

Chapter 02

시제

GRAMMAR FOCUS

1 현재시제

현재의 사실, 습관이나 반복적인 일, 불변의 진리를 나타낼 때 쓴다.

My brother **is** 19 years old. 우리 오빠는 19세이다. 〈현재의 사실〉

I **exercise** for thirty minutes every morning. 나는 매일 아침 30분 동안 운동을 한다. 〈습관〉

The Earth **goes** around the Sun. 지구는 태양 주위를 돈다. 〈불변의 진리〉

2 과거시제

과거의 일이나 상태를 나타낼 때 쓰며, 주로 yesterday, last ~, ~ ago 등 과거를 나타내는 표현과 함께 쓰인다.

I **was** glad to meet my old friend *yesterday*. 나는 어제 내 오랜 친구를 만나서 기뻤다.

Sarah **left** the office *an hour ago*. Sarah는 한 시간 전에 퇴근했다.

3 미래시제

(1) **will + 동사원형**: 미래의 일에 대한 예측(~할 것이다)이나 주어의 의지(~하겠다)를 나타낼 때 주로 쓴다.

The package **will arrive** by Friday. 소포가 금요일까지는 도착할 것이다.

I**'ll** help you with your homework. 내가 네 숙제를 도와줄게.

(2) **be going to + 동사원형**: 미래의 일에 대한 예측(~할 것이다)이나 예정된 계획(~할 예정이다)을 나타낼 때 주로 쓴다.

The weather **is going to be** nice this week. 이번 주에는 날씨가 좋을 것이다.

We **are going to take** a science exam tomorrow. 우리는 내일 과학 시험을 볼 예정이다.

plus will vs. be going to

미래의 일에 대한 예측에는 will과 be going to를 모두 쓸 수 있지만, 말하는 순간의 즉흥적 결정은 will, 예정된 계획은 be going to를 쓴다.

It's too bright in here. I**'ll** draw the curtains. 여기는 너무 밝아. 내가 커튼을 칠게. 〈즉흥적 결정〉

We **are going to** attend the concert on Saturday. 우리는 토요일에 콘서트에 참석할 예정이다. 〈예정된 계획〉

EXERCISE
A

괄호 안에서 알맞은 것을 고르시오.

1 There (are, were) twelve months in a year.

2 I (feel, felt) very hungry now.

3 They (clean, cleaned) the classroom yesterday.

4 The kids (played, will play) soccer a few hours ago.

5 The phone is ringing. I (answer, will answer) it.

6 We are going (have, to have) a party next week.

7 Sam has a good habit; he (reads, read) a book every day.

EXERCISE B

다음 문장을 괄호 안의 지시대로 바꿔 쓰시오.

1 Jack goes jogging in the morning. (과거시제)

→ _____

2 My dad washed his car in the garage. (현재시제)

→ _____

3 Leo will buy tickets to the opera. (과거시제)

→ _____

4 I play tennis with my friends. (미래시제)

→ _____

5 It is going to rain this afternoon. (과거시제)

→ _____

6 The teachers met to discuss the problem. (미래시제)

→ _____

EXERCISE C

괄호 안의 말을 이용하여 문장을 완성하시오.

1 I _____ home all day yesterday. (stay)

2 They _____ an important exam last week. (take)

3 A triangle _____ of three sides. (consist)

4 My grandmother _____ born in 1959. (be)

5 Mary is tall and _____ long, curly hair. (have)

6 The new restaurant on Main Street will _____ soon. (open)

7 I _____ the news about her wedding a few days ago. (hear)

8 The students are going _____ on a field trip next Friday. (go)

9 The doorbell _____, and the baby woke up. (ring)

10 The library opens at 9 a.m. and _____ at 8 p.m. on weekdays. (close)

11 A: I forgot my umbrella.

B: Don't worry. I'll _____ you mine. (lend)

WRITING FOCUS

A 배열 영작   우리말과 일치하도록 괄호 안의 말을 바르게 배열하시오.

1 나의 형은 아침 7시쯤에 일어난다. (my, gets up, 7 o'clock, brother, around)

→ _____ in the morning.

2 목성은 태양계에서 가장 큰 행성이다. (is, Jupiter, biggest, the, planet)

→ _____ in the solar system.

3 우리는 한참 동안 그 버스를 기다렸다. (the, waited, we, for, bus)

→ _____ for a long time.

4 그녀는 자신의 친구들을 파티에 초대했다. (she, her, invited, friends)

→ _____ to the party.

5 그들은 곧 이 도시를 떠날 것이다. (leave, they, city, will, this)

→ _____ soon.

6 그들은 방과 후에 Jim의 집에 갈 것이다. (are, to, go, they, to, going, Jim's house)

→ _____ after school.

B 빈칸 완성   우리말과 일치하도록 빈칸에 알맞은 말을 쓰시오.

1 그들은 일주일에 한 번씩 골프를 친다. (play golf)

→ They _____ _____ once a week.

2 그녀는 해산물을 매우 좋아한다. (like, seafood)

→ She _____ _____ very much.

3 그는 이틀 전에 세미나를 위해 보스턴을 방문했다. (visit, Boston)

→ He _____ _____ for a seminar two days ago.

4 우리 가족은 지난 주말에 캠핑을 갔다. (go camping)

→ My family _____ _____ last weekend.

5 Clara는 우리에게 그녀의 차를 빌려줄 것이다. (lend)

→ Clara _____ _____ her car to us.

6 내일은 눈이 올 것이다. (snow)

→ It _____ _____ _____ _____ tomorrow.

C 문장 완성   우리말과 일치하도록 괄호 안의 말을 이용하여 문장을 완성하시오.

1 그녀는 퇴근 후에 체육관에 간다. (go to the gym)

→ _____ after work.

2 Jennifer는 취미로 사진을 찍는다. (take photographs)

→ _____ as a hobby.

3 나는 그 식당에서 파스타를 주문했다. (order, pasta)

→ _____ at the restaurant.

4 그는 욕실에서 샤워를 했다. (take a shower)

→ _____ in the bathroom.

5 그는 내년에 유럽으로 여행을 갈 것이다. (travel to Europe)

→ _____ next year.

6 우리는 정원에 더 많은 나무를 심을 것이다. (plant, more trees)

→ _____ in the garden.

D 오류 수정   밑줄 친 부분을 바르게 고쳐 문장을 다시 쓰시오.

1 Fruits and vegetables <u>were</u> rich in vitamins.

→ _____

2 Oliver <u>play</u> computer games every evening.

→ _____

3 I <u>watch</u> an action movie on TV yesterday.

→ _____

4 The Berlin Wall <u>falls</u> in 1989.

→ _____

5 He will <u>goes</u> back to school next semester.

→ _____

6 My aunt is going <u>get</u> married next year.

→ _____

현재진행형, 과거진행형

GRAMMAR FOCUS

1 현재진행형

'~하고 있다, ~하는 중이다'의 의미로 지금 진행 중인 동작을 나타내며, 「am/is/are + 동사원형-ing」 형태로 쓴다.

I **am trying** to lose weight. 나는 살을 빼려고 노력하고 있다.

The girl **is picking** up some trash. 그 여자아이는 쓰레기를 줍고 있다.

People **are waiting** in line at the ticket booth. 사람들이 매표소에서 줄을 서서 기다리고 있다.

> **plus** 현재진행형은 가까운 미래에 이미 예정된 계획을 나타낼 때도 쓸 수 있다.
>
> We **are flying** to New York tonight. 우리는 오늘 밤에 비행기를 타고 뉴욕에 갈 예정이다.
>
> (= We **are going to fly** to New York tonight.)

2 과거진행형

'~하고 있었다'의 의미로 과거의 특정 시점에 진행 중이었던 일을 나타내며, 「was/were + 동사원형-ing」 형태로 쓴다.

I **was reading** a book in the library an hour ago. 나는 한 시간 전에 도서관에서 책을 읽고 있었다.

They **were playing** soccer when it started raining. 그들은 비가 내리기 시작했을 때 축구를 하고 있었다.

> *cf.* love, like, want, know, believe, see, taste, have, own, belong to 등 상태와 소유를 나타내는 동사는 진행형으로 쓸 수 없다.
>
> I **have** two movie tickets. 나는 영화표 두 장을 갖고 있다.
> └ am having (×)
>
> He **knew** the truth then. 그는 그때 진실을 알고 있었다.
> └ was knowing (×)

EXERCISE A

괄호 안에서 알맞은 것을 고르시오.

1 A girl (crosses, is crossing) the road right now.

2 Sue (is, was) shopping online for a backpack last night.

3 This sandwich (isn't tasting, doesn't taste) very good.

4 We (are, were) waiting for John to come now.

5 I (am, was) not listening to the radio then.

6 The students (study, were studying) when the teacher came in.

7 They (don't know, aren't knowing) each other's name.

8 We (arrive, are arriving) at the airport in an hour.

9 My brother (is, was) sleeping while I was watching TV.

10 Richard (has, is having) a beautiful house by the beach.

EXERCISE B

밑줄 친 부분을 바르게 고쳐 문장을 다시 쓰시오.

1 Jenny and Amy <u>were</u> shopping at the mall now.

→ _____

2 The hair salon <u>is closing</u> every Tuesday.

→ _____

3 They <u>are</u> practicing serves when their coach arrived.

→ _____

4 She <u>was</u> starting a new job next week.

→ _____

5 We <u>are</u> dancing to the music at that time.

→ _____

6 The kids <u>are wanting</u> to have pizza for dinner.

→ _____

7 Kevin <u>was</u> studying in his room right now.

→ _____

EXERCISE C

〈보기〉에서 알맞은 말을 골라 진행형으로 바꿔 문장을 완성하시오. (단, 한 번씩만 쓸 것)

| 보기 | try | write | listen | go | have | jog | talk | leave |

1 Last night, I _____ on the phone with Jane.

2 They _____ to music in the room right now.

3 All the students _____ their essays now.

4 Steve _____ to finish reading the book last week.

5 We _____ dinner when the doorbell rang.

6 I _____ in the park yesterday afternoon.

7 She _____ for New York tonight. Everything is ready.

8 I _____ to the grocery store in a few minutes.

WRITING FOCUS

A 배열 영작 우리말과 일치하도록 괄호 안의 말을 바르게 배열하시오.

1 나는 내 친구에게 이메일을 쓰고 있다. (am, I, an, writing, email)

→ ＿＿＿＿＿＿＿＿＿＿＿＿＿＿＿＿＿＿ to my friend.

2 Mike는 그의 어머니와 함께 유럽을 여행하고 있다. (traveling, Mike, in, is, Europe)

→ ＿＿＿＿＿＿＿＿＿＿＿＿＿＿＿＿＿＿ with his mother.

3 우리는 함께 수학 문제를 풀고 있다. (are, solving, we, math problems)

→ ＿＿＿＿＿＿＿＿＿＿＿＿＿＿＿＿＿＿ together.

4 Judy는 시험을 위해 그녀의 교과서를 읽고 있었다. (Judy, her, was, textbook, reading)

→ ＿＿＿＿＿＿＿＿＿＿＿＿＿＿＿＿＿＿ for the exam.

5 사람들은 무대 위의 가수를 보고 있었다. (singer, were, people, the, watching)

→ ＿＿＿＿＿＿＿＿＿＿＿＿＿＿＿＿＿＿ on stage.

6 그 남자들은 레슬링 경기에 관해 이야기하고 있었다. (men, talking, the, were, about)

→ ＿＿＿＿＿＿＿＿＿＿＿＿＿＿＿＿＿＿ the wrestling match.

B 빈칸 완성 우리말과 일치하도록 괄호 안의 말을 이용하여 빈칸에 알맞은 말을 쓰시오.

1 그는 파스타에 더 많은 소스를 넣고 있다. (add)

→ He ＿＿＿＿＿ ＿＿＿＿＿ more sauce to the pasta.

2 그녀는 새 노트북을 원한다. (want)

→ She ＿＿＿＿＿ a new laptop.

3 그 남자아이들은 시냇가에서 개구리들을 찾고 있었다. (look)

→ The boys ＿＿＿＿＿ ＿＿＿＿＿ for frogs in the stream.

4 우리는 지금 토론을 하고 있다. (have)

→ We ＿＿＿＿＿ ＿＿＿＿＿ a discussion at the moment.

5 그 아이는 방 안에서 울고 있었다. (cry)

→ The child ＿＿＿＿＿ ＿＿＿＿＿ in the room.

6 수미는 이번 주말에 치과에 갈 예정이다. (go)

→ Sumi ＿＿＿＿＿ ＿＿＿＿＿ to the dentist this weekend.

C 문장 완성 우리말과 일치하도록 괄호 안의 말을 이용하여 문장을 완성하시오.

1 나는 비스킷 위에 버터를 바르고 있다. (spread, butter)

→ I _____ on biscuits.

2 Frank는 사다리를 내려오고 있다. (climb down, the ladder)

→ Frank _____ .

3 Jane은 그녀의 코트에 단추를 꿰매고 있었다. (sew, a button)

→ Jane _____ on her coat.

4 내 남동생과 나는 배드민턴을 치고 있었다. (play, badminton)

→ My brother and I _____ .

5 이 오래된 시계는 나의 할아버지의 것이다. (belong to, my grandfather)

→ This old watch _____ .

6 그들은 내일 아침에 부산으로 떠날 예정이다. (leave for, Busan)

→ They _____ tomorrow morning.

D 오류 수정 어법상 틀린 부분을 바르게 고쳐 문장을 다시 쓰시오.

1 He was driving to work now. (그는 지금 운전해서 출근 중이다.)

→ _____

2 Mom is making dinner for us every day. (엄마는 매일 우리에게 저녁을 만들어 주신다.)

→ _____

3 I am going to the library when I met Steve. (나는 Steve를 만났을 때 도서관에 가는 중이었다.)

→ _____

4 She does her homework an hour ago. (그녀는 한 시간 전에 숙제를 하고 있었다.)

→ _____

5 I am hating winter because of the cold. (나는 추위 때문에 겨울이 싫다.)

→ _____

6 The man was knowing my name. (그 남자는 내 이름을 알고 있었다.)

→ _____

GRAMMAR FOCUS

① 현재완료

「have/has + p.p.」의 형태로, 과거에 일어난 일이 현재까지 영향을 미치거나 지속된 상태를 나타낸다.

긍정문	have/has + p.p.
부정문	have/has + not + p.p.
의문문	Have/Has + 주어 + p.p. ~?

He **has worked** at this company for ten years.
그는 이 회사에서 10년 동안 일해 왔다.

I **have not[haven't] received** an email from you.
저는 당신으로부터 이메일을 받지 못했습니다.

A: **Have** you ever **met** John? John을 만나 본 적이 있니?
B: Yes, I **have**. / No, I **haven't**. 응, 있어. / 아니, 없어.

cf. 현재완료는 yesterday, last ~, ~ ago, when ~ 등 명백한 과거 시점을 나타내는 표현과 함께 쓸 수 없다.

He **graduated** from college *three years ago*. 그는 3년 전에 대학을 졸업했다.
└ has graduated (×)

② 현재완료의 용법

(1) 완료: '(방금/이미) ~했다'의 의미로, 과거에 시작된 일이 현재는 완료된 상태임을 나타낸다. 주로 just(방금), already(이미), yet(아직) 등과 함께 쓰인다.

We **have** *just* **finished** cleaning up the room. 우리는 방금 방 치우는 것을 끝냈다.

(2) 경험: '~한 적이 있다'의 의미로, 현재까지의 경험을 나타낸다. 주로 ever(지금까지), never(한 번도 ~ 않다), once(한 번), twice(두 번), many times(여러 번), before(전에) 등과 함께 쓰인다.

I **have** *never* **traveled** abroad. 나는 해외를 한 번도 여행해 본 적이 없다.

(3) 결과: '~했다'의 의미로, 과거에 일어난 일의 결과가 현재에도 남아 있음을 나타낸다.

Kevin **has gone** to Paris. Kevin은 파리로 갔다. (현재 여기에 없음)

cf. Kevin **has been** to Paris. Kevin은 파리에 가 본 적이 있다. 〈경험〉

(4) 계속: '(지금까지 계속) ~해 왔다'의 의미로, 과거에 시작된 일이 현재까지 계속된 상태임을 나타낸다. 「for + 기간」(~ 동안), 「since + 시점」(~ 이후로), how long ~(얼마나 오랫동안) 등과 함께 쓰인다.

I **have lived** in this neighborhood *for five years*. 나는 이 동네에서 5년 동안 살아왔다.

EXERCISE A

괄호 안의 말을 이용하여 현재완료 문장을 완성하시오.

1 I _____ _____ him on TV before. (see)

2 Sarah _____ _____ the book three times. (read)

3 We _____ just _____ at the airport. (arrive)

4 She _____ _____ in this city for four years. (live)

5 Joshua _____ _____ his wallet at home. (leave)

EXERCISE B

다음 문장을 밑줄 친 부분에 주의하여 우리말로 해석하시오.

1 We have already cleaned the house.

→ _____

2 Bill hasn't done his homework yet.

→ _____

3 I have eaten Mexican food many times.

→ _____

4 They have gone to the United States.

→ _____

5 She has been to London before.

→ _____

6 We have lived in this house since 2020.

→ _____

EXERCISE C

다음 문장을 현재완료를 사용하여 한 문장으로 바꿀 때, 빈칸에 알맞은 말을 쓰시오.

1 Ted lost his watch. He still doesn't have it now.

→ Ted _____ _____ his watch.

2 They went to Florida a few months ago. They are not here any longer.

→ They _____ _____ to Florida.

3 She moved to Seoul five years ago. She lives in Seoul now.

→ She _____ _____ in Seoul for five years.

4 I started studying Chinese two years ago. I still study Chinese.

→ I _____ _____ Chinese for two years.

5 We became friends during our childhood. We are still friends.

→ We _____ _____ friends since childhood.

6 The pond froze over last week. It is still frozen over.

→ The pond _____ _____ _____ since last week.

WRITING FOCUS

A 배열 영작 우리말과 일치하도록 괄호 안의 말을 바르게 배열하시오.

1 Mary는 10년 동안 영어를 가르쳐 왔다. (taught, ten years, has, Mary, for, English)

→ _____

2 나의 호주인 친구는 한국으로 이주했다. (has, to, moved, my Australian friend, Korea)

→ _____

3 그 구급차는 아직 도착하지 않았다. (has, the, yet, ambulance, arrived, not)

→ _____

4 그녀는 싱가포르에 한 번도 가 본 적이 없다. (never, to, has, she, been, Singapore)

→ _____

5 그 기차는 이미 그 역을 출발했다. (the, already, the, has, train, left, station)

→ _____

6 당신은 자유의 여신상을 본 적이 있습니까? (have, seen, you, ever, the Statue of Liberty)

→ _____

B 빈칸 완성 우리말과 일치하도록 괄호 안의 말을 이용하여 빈칸에 알맞은 말을 쓰시오.

1 그 우유는 상했다. (go bad)

→ The milk _____ _____ _____.

2 Alberto는 그리스에 두 번 가 봤다. (Greece)

→ Alberto _____ _____ _____ _____ twice.

3 그들은 방금 아침 식사를 끝냈다. (just, finish)

→ They _____ _____ _____ breakfast.

4 당신은 얼마나 오랫동안 여기서 살았습니까? (live)

→ How long _____ _____ _____ here?

5 그는 수영하는 법을 한 번도 배운 적이 없다. (learn)

→ He _____ _____ _____ how to swim.

6 그녀는 열 다섯 살 때부터 안경을 써 왔다. (wear)

→ She _____ _____ glasses since she was fifteen.

C 문장 완성   우리말과 일치하도록 괄호 안의 말을 이용하여 문장을 완성하시오. (단, 현재완료를 사용할 것)

1 Mark와 Emily는 유치원 때부터 서로 알고 지냈다. (know each other, kindergarten)

→ Mark and Emily _____ .

2 당신은 얼마나 오랫동안 그 오토바이를 타셨습니까? (drive)

→ _____ the motorcycle?

3 나는 내 오래된 청바지를 내다 버렸다. (throw away)

→ _____ my old jeans.

4 James는 그 소설을 열 번 이상 읽었다. (read, the novel)

→ _____ more than ten times.

5 우리는 이미 전기 요금을 납부했다. (already, pay)

→ _____ the electricity bill.

6 당신은 스페인 음식을 먹어 본 적이 있나요? (ever, try)

→ _____ Spanish food?

D 오류 수정   어법상 틀린 부분을 바르게 고쳐 문장을 다시 쓰시오.

1 He has never gone to Korea. (그는 한국에 가 본 적이 없다.)

→ _____

2 How long did you studied English? (당신은 얼마나 오랫동안 영어를 공부해 왔습니까?)

→ _____

3 We didn't arrived at the park yet. (우리는 아직 공원에 도착하지 못했다.)

→ _____

4 She have read fifteen books so far this year. (그녀는 올해 지금까지 책 열 다섯 권을 읽었다.)

→ _____

5 I have left my keys at home yesterday. (나는 어제 내 열쇠를 집에 두고 왔다.)

→ _____

6 He has worked at the same company since five years. (그는 5년 동안 같은 회사에서 일해 왔다.)

→ _____

[01-02] 빈칸에 들어갈 말로 알맞은 것을 고르시오.

01

The moon _____ around the Earth.

① goes
② went
③ will go
④ is going
⑤ has gone

02

All the guests _____ the cake a lot at the party last night.

① like
② liked
③ are liking
④ were liking
⑤ have liked

03 빈칸에 들어갈 말이 순서대로 짝지어진 것은?

• He _____ up at 7 o'clock these days.
• I _____ my cousin in New York next summer.

① wakes – visit
② woke – visited
③ woke – will visit
④ wakes – will visit
⑤ will wake – am visiting

04 우리말과 일치하도록 주어진 말을 배열할 때, 네 번째로 오는 단어는?

그들은 새 아파트로 이사할 예정이다.
(apartment, to, they, new, are, move, a, to, going)

① a
② to
③ are
④ move
⑤ going

05 밑줄 친 부분의 쓰임이 나머지 넷과 다른 것은?

① She <u>has eaten</u> sushi twice.
② <u>Have</u> you ever <u>been</u> to Europe?
③ I've <u>eaten</u> at this restaurant before.
④ My dad <u>has gone</u> to Japan for work.
⑤ She <u>has</u> never <u>ridden</u> a roller coaster.

06 다음 중 대화가 자연스럽지 <u>않은</u> 것은?

① A: Have you seen the new movie?
　 B: Yes, I watched it last weekend.
② A: What is Tom doing now?
　 B: He goes to the gym.
③ A: When will you begin this work?
　 B: Sometime next week.
④ A: What did you do last weekend?
　 B: I went to the art exhibition.
⑤ A: What were you doing yesterday evening?
　 B: I was writing a report in the library.

빈출
07 다음 중 어법상 올바른 것은?

① When have you studied abroad?
② I have lost three kilograms last year.
③ My car has broken down a week ago.
④ We have known each other for four years.
⑤ They have been to the Eiffel Tower in 2019.

고난도
08 어법상 <u>틀린</u> 문장을 <u>모두</u> 고르면?

ⓐ Are you going for a walk?
ⓑ I have not done the laundry yet.
ⓒ Ocean water contains a lot of salt.
ⓓ This book is belonging to the library.
ⓔ He has practiced yoga since five years.

① ⓐ, ⓒ
② ⓐ, ⓔ
③ ⓑ, ⓒ
④ ⓒ, ⓓ
⑤ ⓓ, ⓔ

✎ 서술형

09 우리말과 일치하도록 주어진 말을 바르게 배열하시오.

(1) 경찰이 방금 현장에 도착했다. (the, just, on, the, have, police, scene, arrived)

→ _____

(2) 당신은 베를린에서 얼마나 오래 살았나요?
(lived, have, how, you, in, long, Berlin)

→ _____

10 빈칸에 들어갈 말을 〈보기〉에서 골라 알맞은 형태로 쓰시오.

보기	finish	happen	rent

(1) We _____ a car after we arrived at the airport.

(2) February 29 only _____ once every four years.

(3) She _____ writing her book by next month.

11 주어진 문장을 지시에 맞게 바꿔 쓰시오.

(1) Nicole tries to find a job. (현재진행형으로)

→ _____

(2) They sat in the very back of the bus.
(과거진행형으로)

→ _____

12 두 문장을 현재완료를 사용하여 한 문장으로 바꿔 쓰시오.

(1) I forgot your name. I can't remember it now.

→ I _____ .

(2) Mary joined the book club six months ago.
She is still a member of the book club.

→ Mary _____

_____ six months.

13 어법상 틀린 부분을 찾아 바르게 고치시오.

(1) I am knowing Mr. Smith very well.

_____ → _____

(2) She has won the best actress award at Cannes in 2003.

_____ → _____

14 밑줄 친 우리말과 일치하도록 주어진 말을 활용하여 문장을 완성하시오.

A: 저는 뉴질랜드에 한 번도 가 본 적이 없어요.
(never, New Zealand)

B: It is a beautiful country. You should go.

→ _____

15 우리말과 일치하도록 주어진 말을 활용하여 문장을 완성하시오.

(1) 그들은 해변에서 모래성을 쌓고 있었다.
(build, a sandcastle)

→ They _____
on the beach.

(2) 그는 이미 커피를 세 잔 마셨다. (already, drink)

→ He _____
three cups of coffee.

16 일기예보를 보고, 〈조건〉에 맞게 문장을 완성하시오.

Date	Boston	California
May 4		
May 5 (Today)		
May 6		

조건 1. cloudy, rainy, sunny, windy 중 한 단어를 사용할 것
2. 알맞은 시제를 사용할 것

(1) It _____ _____ in Boston yesterday.

(2) It _____ _____ _____ in Boston tomorrow.

(3) It _____ _____ in California since yesterday.

17 Angela의 오후 일과표를 보고, 질문에 대한 답을 쓰시오.

4:00	do her homework
6:30	have dinner
8:00	walk her dog
9:00	watch TV
10:00	go to bed

Q: It is 8:00 p.m. now. What is Angela doing?

A: She (1) _____.

Q: What was Angela doing at 4:00 p.m. this afternoon?

A: She (2) _____ at that time.

18 대화를 읽고, 어법상 맞는 것을 괄호 안에서 골라 각각 쓰시오.

A: Luke, (1) (did you ever watch / have you ever watched) a Korean movie?

B: Yes, I have. I (2) (watched / have watched) my first Korean movie two years ago. It was difficult to understand back then, but now I (3) (enjoy / enjoyed) watching Korean movies.

A: That's amazing. I (4) (have / am having) two tickets for a Korean movie. Would you like to come with me?

B: Sure. I'd love to go.

(1) _____   (2) _____

(3) _____   (4) _____

[19-20] 다음 글을 읽고, 물음에 답하시오.

Hi, I'm Mina. I ⓐcame to England to learn English last year, and I ⓑam staying in Cambridge now. 저는 이곳에 도착한 이후로 영국의 많은 곳을 방문했어요. For example, London is a large city with many interesting things to see. I ⓒhave already tried the famous fish and chips, but I ⓓdidn't have shepherd's pie yet. I ⓔam going to try it this Sunday.

19 밑줄 친 우리말과 일치하도록 〈조건〉에 맞게 문장을 완성하시오.

조건 arrive, visit를 활용할 것

→ Since I _____ here, I _____ many places in the U.K.

20 어법상 틀린 것을 찾아 기호를 쓰고 바르게 고치시오.

(_____) → _____

Chapter
03

조동사

능력, 추측, 허가, 요청

조동사는 동사 앞에 쓰여 능력, 추측, 허가, 의무, 조언 등의 의미를 더해 주는 말이다. 조동사는 주어의 인칭과 수에 관계없이 형태가 같으며, 뒤에 항상 동사원형을 쓴다.

1 능력을 나타내는 조동사

can	~할 수 있다	I **can** play the guitar very well. He **cannot[can't]** see without his glasses. (~할 수 없다) A: **Can** you drive a car? B: Yes, I **can**. / No, I **can't**.
could	~할 수 있었다	He **could** run faster years ago. She **couldn't** stop laughing. (~할 수 없었다)
be able to	~할 수 있(었)다	I **am able to** swim 500 meters. We **were able to** catch the train.

plus 조동사는 두 개를 나란히 쓸 수 없으며, '~할 수 있을 것이다'는 will be able to로 쓴다.

I **will be able to** finish the report tomorrow.
└─ will can (×)

2 추측을 나타내는 조동사

may, might	~일지도 모른다	It **may**(= **might**) rain this weekend. She **may**(= **might**) **not** like the gift. (~이 아닐지도 모른다)
must	~임에 틀림없다	It's past 11:00 p.m. The store **must** be closed.
cannot	~일 리가 없다	The rumor **cannot[can't]** be true. It's unbelievable.

3 허가를 나타내는 조동사

can, may	~해도 좋다	You **can** borrow my book. You **may** take a break if you need to.
Can / Could / May I ~?	~해도 될까요?	A: **Can[Could / May] I** use this pen? B: Yes, you **can[could / may]**. *Could / May가 Can보다 정중한 표현

4 요청을 나타내는 조동사

Can / Could / Will / Would you ~?	~해 주시겠어요?	A: **Can[Could / Will / Would] you** pass me the salt? B: Sure. / Certainly. *Could / Would가 Can / Will보다 정중한 표현

cf. May you ~?는 쓰지 않는다.

EXERCISE A

괄호 안에서 알맞은 것을 고르시오.

1 He can (speak, speaks) three languages.

2 She will (can, be able to) find a job soon.

3 David is a genius. He must (know, to know) the answer.

4 I (may, can) go to the party, but I'm not sure yet.

5 (May, Would) I borrow your pen for a moment?

6 (May, Could) you show me your ID?

EXERCISE B

우리말과 일치하도록 밑줄 친 부분을 바르게 고치시오.

1 그녀는 어디에서도 자신의 안경을 찾을 수 없었다.

→ She <u>can't</u> find her glasses anywhere.

2 나는 다음 달에 내 사촌을 만나러 캐나다에 갈지도 모른다.

→ I <u>must</u> go to Canada to visit my cousin next month.

3 그는 미국인이 아닐지도 모른다.

→ He <u>may be not</u> American.

4 Jane, 나와 결혼해 줄래요?

→ Jane, <u>do you will</u> marry me?

EXERCISE C

〈보기〉에서 알맞은 조동사를 고른 후, 괄호 안의 동사를 함께 써서 대화를 완성하시오.

보기	can	may	must

1 A: _____ I _____ your laptop? Mine is too slow. (use)

B: Yes, you may. I don't need it now.

2 A: _____ you _____ any musical instruments? (play)

B: Yes, I can play the cello. I learned to play it for four years.

3 A: I prepared a big dinner, but Jack isn't eating any food.

B: He ate a large pizza by himself. He _____ _____ full. (be)

WRITING FOCUS

A 배열 영작   우리말과 일치하도록 괄호 안의 말을 바르게 배열하시오.

1 그는 지금 매우 피곤한 것이 틀림없다. (must, he, be, tired, now, very)

→ _____

2 제가 오늘 일찍 퇴근해도 될까요? (leave, early, I, can, today)

→ _____

3 그녀는 이탈리아 음식을 아주 잘 만들 수 있다. (she, Italian food, make, can, very well)

→ _____

4 나에게 네 공책 좀 빌려주겠니? (could, me, lend, your, you, notebook)

→ _____

5 Paul은 내 생일 파티에 오지 않을지도 모른다. (may, Paul, my, come, not, to, birthday party)

→ _____

6 나는 극장에서 자리를 잡을 수 있었다. (was, at, a seat, to, able, I, take, the theater)

→ _____

B 빈칸 완성   우리말과 일치하도록 괄호 안의 말을 이용하여 빈칸에 알맞은 말을 쓰시오.

1 제가 창문을 열어도 될까요? (open, may)

→ _____ _____ _____ the window?

2 문에 누군가 있는 것이 틀림없다. (be, must)

→ There _____ _____ someone at the door.

3 내 부탁 하나만 들어 줄래? (do, will)

→ _____ _____ _____ me a favor?

4 그는 자신의 사무실에 없을지도 모른다. (be, may)

→ He _____ _____ _____ in his office.

5 나는 어젯밤에 천둥 번개 때문에 잠을 잘 수가 없었다. (sleep, can)

→ I _____ _____ last night because of the thunder and lightning.

6 Jack은 100미터를 13초에 달릴 수 있다. (run, be able to)

→ Jack _____ _____ _____ _____ 100 meters in 13 seconds.

C 문장 완성   우리말과 일치하도록 괄호 안의 말을 이용하여 문장을 완성하시오.

1 그들은 부부임에 틀림없다. (a couple, must)

➡ _____

2 제가 당신의 여권을 봐도 될까요? (see, passport, may)

➡ _____

3 그는 강을 건너 수영할 수 있었다. (swim, across the river, be able to)

➡ _____

4 너는 윗몸 일으키기를 할 수 있니? (do sit-ups, can)

➡ _____

5 우리는 그 문제를 해결하지 못할지도 모른다. (solve, the problem, might)

➡ _____

6 문 좀 닫아 주시겠어요? (close, the door, could)

➡ _____

D 오류 수정   밑줄 친 부분을 바르게 고쳐 문장을 다시 쓰시오.

1 My brother can plays the drums. (나의 형은 드럼을 연주할 수 있다.)

➡ _____

2 Amy may like not horror movies. (Amy는 공포 영화를 좋아하지 않지도 모른다.)

➡ _____

3 We could heard his voice very clearly. (우리는 그의 목소리를 매우 또렷하게 들을 수 있었다.)

➡ _____

4 Did you able to find the restaurant? (당신은 그 식당을 찾을 수 있었습니까?)

➡ _____

5 This must is Sally's scarf. (이것은 Sally의 스카프인 것이 틀림없다.)

➡ _____

6 Tom will can drive next year. (Tom은 내년이면 운전을 할 수 있을 것이다.)

➡ _____

1 의무를 나타내는 조동사

must	~해야 한다 〈의무〉	Drivers **must**(= **have to**) follow the traffic rules.
	~해서는 안 된다 〈금지〉	You **must not** press the red button.
have to	~해야 한다 〈의무〉	She **has to**(= **must**) take her medicine every day. ＊주어가 3인칭 단수일 때: has to
	~할 필요가 없다 〈불필요〉	You **don't have to** take off your shoes here.

> **plus** must가 의무를 나타낼 때 미래형은 will have to, 과거형은 had to를 쓴다.
>
> The team **will have to** work overtime next week. 그 팀은 다음 주에 초과 근무를 해야 할 것이다.
>
> I **had to** go to the dentist last Friday. 나는 지난주 금요일에 치과에 가야 했다.

2 조언을 나타내는 조동사

should, ought to	~해야 한다 〈조언〉	He **should**(= **ought to**) get some rest. You **shouldn't**(= **ought not to**) skip meals. (~해서는 안 된다)
had better	~하는 것이 좋겠다 〈경고〉	We **had better** leave now to avoid traffic. She **had better not** be late for school anymore. (~하지 않는 것이 좋겠다)

3 과거의 습관을 나타내는 조동사

used to	~하곤 했다 〈과거의 습관〉	I **used to**(= **would**) jog every morning, but I don't anymore.
	~였다 〈과거의 상태〉	There **used to** be a big tree in the backyard. ＊과거의 상태는 would로 바꿔 쓸 수 없다.

EXERCISE A

괄호 안에서 알맞은 것을 고르시오.

1 The baby is sleeping. We (must, must not) make any noise.

2 The roads are icy. You (should, shouldn't) drive slowly.

3 She used to (eat, eating) meat, but now she is a vegetarian.

4 It will rain later today. You (had better, used to) take an umbrella.

5 I (don't have to, must) wake up early tomorrow. It's a holiday.

6 Chris (has to, had to) drive his mother to the airport yesterday.

EXERCISE B

우리말과 일치하도록 밑줄 친 부분을 바르게 고치시오.

1 그녀는 6개월마다 건강 검진을 받아야 한다.

→ She <u>have to</u> have a check-up every six months.

2 너는 파티에 아무 것도 가져올 필요가 없다.

→ You <u>must not</u> bring anything to the party.

3 그는 취업 면접에 늦지 않는 것이 좋겠다.

→ He <u>had not better</u> be late for his job interview.

4 우리 할아버지는 그 전쟁 중에 비행기 조종사였다.

→ My grandfather <u>would</u> be a pilot during the war.

EXERCISE C

〈보기〉에서 알맞은 동사를 고른 후, 괄호 안의 조동사를 함께 써서 대화를 완성하시오.

보기	go	pay	take

1 A: I have a sore throat. It hurts when I speak.

B: I think you _____ _____ to the doctor right away. (should)

2 A: You _____ _____ _____ any pictures in the museum. (must)

B: Oh, I didn't know that. I will put my camera in the bag.

3 A: How much are tickets for the event?

B: You _____ _____ _____ _____ for tickets.

The event is free. (have to)

WRITING FOCUS

A 배열 영작　우리말과 일치하도록 괄호 안의 말을 바르게 배열하시오.

1 건강을 위해서는 규칙적으로 운동해야 한다. (work out, you, regularly, should)

→ _____ for your health.

2 학생들은 수업에 그들의 교과서를 가져와야 한다. (their, bring, students, must, textbooks)

→ _____ to class.

3 너는 그 일에 대해 걱정할 필요가 없어. (don't, you, have, worry, to)

→ _____ about the matter.

4 Lisa는 방콕에서 여행 가이드로 일했었다. (Lisa, work, a, to, as, used, tour guide)

→ _____ in Bangkok.

5 우리는 표를 구하기 위해 줄을 서서 기다려야 했다. (we, wait, to, in line, had)

→ _____ to get the tickets.

6 너는 커피에 더 많은 설탕을 넣지 않는 게 좋겠어. (not, had, sugar, better, you, add, more)

→ _____ to the coffee.

B 빈칸 완성　우리말과 일치하도록 괄호 안의 말을 이용하여 빈칸에 알맞은 말을 쓰시오.

1 그것은 훌륭한 영화야. 너는 그것을 봐야 해. (watch, should)

→ It is a great movie. You _____ _____ it.

2 우리는 그 돈을 한 번에 모두 쓰지 말아야 한다. (spend, ought to)

→ We _____ _____ _____ _____ all the money at once.

3 그는 오늘 출근할 필요가 없다. (go, have to)

→ He _____ _____ _____ _____ to work today.

4 너는 수업 시간에 네 휴대폰을 사용해서는 안 된다. (use, must)

→ You _____ _____ _____ your cellphone in class.

5 우리는 해변에서 조개껍데기를 줍곤 했다. (collect, would)

→ We _____ _____ seashells on the beach.

6 너무 늦었으니 우리는 택시를 타는 것이 좋겠어. (take, had better)

→ It's too late, so we _____ _____ _____ a taxi.

C 문장 완성   우리말과 일치하도록 괄호 안의 말을 이용하여 문장을 완성하시오.

1 전 직원은 안전모를 착용해야 한다. (wear, safety helmets, must)

→ All employees _____.

2 너는 빗길에서 조심히 운전하는 게 좋겠어. (drive, carefully, had better)

→ _____ in the rain.

3 모퉁이를 돌면 골동품 가게가 하나 있었다. (there, an antique shop, used to)

→ _____ around the corner.

4 나는 어제 그 재킷을 반품해야 했다. (return, the jacket, have to)

→ _____ yesterday.

5 너는 파티를 위해 옷을 차려 입을 필요가 없어. (dress up, have to)

→ _____ for the party.

6 너는 젖은 손으로 그 전선을 만져서는 안 된다. (touch, the electric wire, must)

→ _____ with wet hands.

D 오류 수정   밑줄 친 부분을 바르게 고쳐 문장을 다시 쓰시오.

1 You must to prepare your passport and plane ticket. (너는 여권과 비행기 표를 준비해야 한다.)

→ _____

2 I must study late last night. (나는 어젯밤에 늦게까지 공부해야 했다.)

→ _____

3 You ought wash your hands after using the restroom. (화장실을 사용한 후에는 손을 씻어야 한다.)

→ _____

4 You don't have to park in the handicapped parking area. (장애인 주차 구역에 주차해서는 안 된다.)

→ _____

5 You have better take a first-aid kit. (너는 구급상자를 가져가는 것이 좋을 거야.)

→ _____

6 I would hate spicy food. (나는 매운 음식을 싫어했었다.)

→ _____

01 대화의 빈칸에 들어갈 말로 알맞은 것은?

> A: Where is Tom?
> B: I am not sure. He _____ be in his room.

① may   ② must   ③ should
④ used to   ⑤ had better

빈출

02 빈칸에 공통으로 들어갈 말은?

> • She is wearing a school uniform. She _____ be a student.
> • You _____ not litter in public places.

① had   ② can   ③ must
④ should   ⑤ have to

03 빈칸에 들어갈 말이 순서대로 짝지어진 것은?

> • You look tired. You _____ get some rest.
> • Eddy is an auto mechanic. He _____ repair cars.

① should – can   ② would – could
③ can – had better   ④ ought to – can't
⑤ have to – used to

04 두 문장을 의미가 같도록 한 문장으로 바꿔 쓸 때, 빈칸에 알맞은 것은?

> I lived in Busan, but I don't live there anymore.
> → I _____ live in Busan.

① will   ② would   ③ used to
④ ought to   ⑤ must not

05 빈칸에 can[Can]이 들어갈 수 없는 것은?

① You _____ take a seat here.
② _____ he speak any other languages?
③ I _____ swim when I was 10 years old.
④ Some animals _____ see well at night.
⑤ _____ you lend me your phone charger?

06 우리말을 영어로 잘못 옮긴 것은?

① 우리는 그 행사에 정장을 입을 필요가 없다.
 → We must not wear a suit to the event.
② 그는 그 수학 문제를 풀 수 있었다.
 → He was able to solve the math problem.
③ 너는 식사 후에 이를 닦아야 한다.
 → You should brush your teeth after meals.
④ 너는 그 의사의 조언을 따르는 것이 좋겠어.
 → You had better follow the doctor's advice.
⑤ 나는 점심시간에 산책을 하곤 했다.
 → I would go for a walk during my lunch break.

07 두 문장의 의미가 서로 다른 것은?

① He can run 10 kilometers.
 = He is able to run 10 kilometers.
② The man cannot be the thief.
 = The man may not be the thief.
③ Can I borrow your tennis racket?
 = May I borrow your tennis racket?
④ We must leave for the airport in an hour.
 = We have to leave for the airport in an hour.
⑤ You should stop worrying about the problem.
 = You ought to stop worrying about the problem.

고난도

08 어법상 올바른 문장의 개수는?

ⓐ They will can visit us tomorrow.
ⓑ You had not better play with fire.
ⓒ Would you please come this way?
ⓓ There would be a church near my house.
ⓔ You must not share your password with anyone.

① 1개　　② 2개　　③ 3개
④ 4개　　⑤ 5개

／ 서술형

09 우리말과 일치하도록 주어진 말을 바르게 배열하시오.

(1) 그녀는 스웨터를 뜰 수 있다.

(to, is, sweater, able, she, a, knit)

→ _____

(2) 그는 자신의 행동에 사과해야 한다.

(he, apologize, ought, behavior, for, to, his)

→ _____

10 〈보기〉에서 알맞은 말을 골라 문장을 완성하시오.
(단, 한 번씩만 쓸 것)

보기	don't have to	had better	used to

(1) He _____ wear a coat. It's cold outside.

(2) You _____ explain. I already understand.

(3) We _____ be neighbors for many years.

---

11 주어진 문장을 지시에 맞게 바꿔 쓰시오.

(1) She must study hard for the exam. (과거시제로)

→ _____

(2) We had better park the car here. (부정문으로)

→ _____

12 우리말과 일치하도록 주어진 말을 사용하여 문장을 완성하시오.

(1) 그 버스는 정시에 출발하지 않을지도 모른다. (leave)

→ The bus _____ _____ _____ on time.

(2) Eric은 겨울에 스키를 타러 가곤 했다. (go skiing)

→ Eric _____ _____ _____ in winter.

빈출

13 어법상 틀린 부분을 찾아 바르게 고치시오.

(1) She must not cook dinner tonight.
(그녀는 오늘 저녁 식사를 요리할 필요가 없다.)

_____ → _____

(2) They may be sisters. They look alike.
(그들은 자매임이 틀림없어. 그들은 닮았어.)

_____ → _____

14 〈보기〉에서 필요한 단어들만 골라 대화를 완성하시오.

보기	can	may	this jar
	I	you	open

A: _____ for me?
B: Sure. Let me give it a try.

15 그림을 보고, 주어진 말을 활용하여 문장을 완성하시오.

(1) STOP

(2)

괄호 안의 말과 must 를 사용할 것

(1) You _____ here. (stop)

(2) You _____ a bike. (ride)

16 각 상자에서 필요한 말을 한 번씩만 써서 문장을 완성하시오.

| may |
| have to |
| would |

| bake |
| go |
| return |

(1) I _____ the book to the library today.

(2) My grandmother _____ pies when we visited her.

(3) She _____ on vacation, but she hasn't decided yet.

17 밑줄 친 우리말과 일치하도록 문장을 완성하시오.

A: Look over there! Isn't that Alex?

B: 저 사람은 Alex일 리가 없어. He moved to a different city last year.

→ That _____ _____ _____.

고난도

18 〈보기〉에 주어진 조동사를 사용하여 글을 완성하시오. (단, 한 번씩만 쓸 것)

| 보기 | can | could | should | would |

Mr. Johnson (1) _____ go jogging every morning. He (2) _____ run about 3 kilometers without taking a break. However, he doesn't go jogging anymore and has gained weight. His doctor says he (3) _____ start exercising again, so he is planning to sign up at a gym. He believes he (4) _____ get back into shape.

[19-20] 대화를 읽고, 물음에 답하시오.

A: I haven't finished my essay yet.

B: Oh, no! You had better to hurry. It's due tomorrow.

A: 나는 그것을 마감일 전에 끝낼 수 없을 것 같아. Can you give me a hand?

B: Of course. I'll help you out.

A: Thank you so much.

19 어법상 틀린 부분을 찾아 바르게 고치시오.

_____ → _____

20 밑줄 친 우리말과 일치하도록 〈조건〉에 맞게 문장을 완성하시오.

1. will, able, finish, it을 사용할 것
2. 8단어를 추가하여 문장을 완성할 것

→ I think _____ before the deadline.

Chapter 04

to부정사

UNIT 01 to부정사의 명사적 용법

GRAMMAR FOCUS

to부정사는 「to + 동사원형」 형태이며, 문장에서 명사, 형용사, 부사처럼 쓰인다.

❶ to부정사의 명사적 용법

to부정사가 명사처럼 쓰여 문장에서 주어, 보어, 목적어 역할을 하며, '~하는 것, ~하기'로 해석한다. 주어로 쓰인
to부정사(구)는 주로 가주어 it으로 대신하고 문장 맨 뒤로 보낸다.

주어	**To solve** the question was impossible. = **It** was impossible **to solve** the question. 가주어 진주어	그 문제를 **푸는 것은** 불가능했다.
보어	My dream is **to buy** a big boat. He wanted me **to be** quiet.	나의 꿈은 큰 배를 **사는 것이다.** 〈주격보어〉 그는 내가 조용히 **있기를** 원했다. 〈목적격보어〉
목적어	I learned **to ski** last winter.	나는 작년 겨울에 **스키 타는 것을** 배웠다.

cf. to부정사를 목적어로 취하는 동사

want, need, hope, expect, plan, promise, decide, learn, wish, fail, agree, refuse 등

❷ 의문사 + to부정사

문장에서 주어, 보어, 목적어로 쓰이며, 「의문사 + 주어 + should + 동사원형」으로 바꿔 쓸 수 있다.

· when + to부정사	언제 ~할지	· what + to부정사	무엇을 ~할지
· where + to부정사	어디서 ~할지	· how + to부정사	어떻게 ~할지, ~하는 방법

I don't know **what to do** now. 나는 지금 **무엇을 해야 할지** 모르겠다.

= I don't know **what I should do** now.

cf. 「why + to부정사」는 쓰지 않는다.

A 괄호 안에서 알맞은 것을 고르시오.

1 He wants (change, to change) jobs.

2 (Make, To make) fun of other people is not nice.

3 My dream is (travel, to travel) around the world.

4 (It, That) is exciting to watch a basketball game.

5 The question is when (starting, to start) the project.

6 You can decide (what, why) to have for dinner.

7 My sister promised (go, to go) to the movies with me.

8 What present do you expect to (get, getting) for your birthday?

EXERCISE B

우리말과 일치하도록 〈보기〉에서 알맞은 말을 골라 문장을 완성하시오. (단, to부정사를 사용할 것)

보기	play	see	speak	start	stop

1 이 매장의 관리자를 만나고 싶습니다.

→ I want ＿＿＿＿＿＿＿ the manager of the shop.

2 많은 청중 앞에서 연설하는 것은 쉽지 않다.

→ It is not easy ＿＿＿＿＿＿＿ in front of a large audience.

3 그의 계획은 자신의 사업을 시작하는 것이다.

→ His plan is ＿＿＿＿＿＿＿ his own business.

4 누가 너에게 기타 치는 법을 가르쳐 주었니?

→ Who taught you how ＿＿＿＿＿＿＿ the guitar?

5 나는 그에게 차를 세우라고 말했다.

→ I told him ＿＿＿＿＿＿＿ the car.

EXERCISE C

우리말과 일치하도록 to부정사를 사용하여 문장을 완성하시오.

1 나는 이 복사기를 사용하는 방법을 모른다.

→ I don't know how ＿＿＿＿＿＿＿ this copy machine.

2 나는 네가 우리 집에 오면 좋겠어.

→ I would like you ＿＿＿＿＿＿＿ over to my place.

3 중국어를 배우는 것은 재미있다.

→ ＿＿＿＿＿＿＿ Chinese is interesting.

4 나는 내 가족과 함께 주말을 보내고 싶다.

→ I hope ＿＿＿＿＿＿＿ the weekend with my family.

5 오늘날 기술 없이 사는 것은 불가능하다.

→ Today, it is impossible ＿＿＿＿＿＿＿ without technology.

6 그들은 더 큰 아파트로 이사를 가기로 계획했다.

→ They planned ＿＿＿＿＿＿＿ to a bigger apartment.

WRITING FOCUS

A 배열 영작   우리말과 일치하도록 괄호 안의 말을 바르게 배열하시오.

1 매일 운동하는 것은 쉽지 않다. (not, it, easy, exercise, is, to)

→ _____ every day.

2 친구들에게 작별 인사를 하는 것은 어렵다. (it, to, say, is, difficult, goodbye)

→ _____ to friends.

3 내 목표는 그 시험에서 만점을 받는 것이다. (my, a, goal, to, is, perfect, get, score)

→ _____ on the exam.

4 네가 곧 우리를 방문하면 좋겠어. (I, you, us, want, visit, to)

→ _____ soon.

5 Tom은 항상 Jerry를 잡는 데 실패한다. (to, fails, catch, Jerry, always)

→ Tom _____ .

6 나의 할머니는 내게 목도리 뜨는 법을 가르쳐 주셨다. (me, to, muffler, taught, a, knit, how)

→ My grandmother _____ .

B 빈칸 완성   우리말과 일치하도록 괄호 안의 말을 이용하여 빈칸에 알맞은 말을 쓰시오.

1 외국어를 정복하는 것은 쉽지 않다. (master)

→ _____ is not easy _____ _____ a foreign language.

2 보는 것이 믿는 것이다. (백문이 불여일견) (see, believe)

→ _____ _____ is _____ _____ .

3 그녀는 나에게 창문을 닫아달라고 부탁했다. (ask, close)

→ She _____ _____ _____ _____ the window.

4 Kate는 그녀의 남동생의 숙제를 도와주기로 승낙했다. (agree, help)

→ Kate _____ _____ _____ her brother with his homework.

5 너는 그에게 사과할 필요가 없다. (need, apologize)

→ You don't _____ _____ _____ to him.

6 Chris는 나에게 내 코트를 어디에 두어야 하는지 알려 주었다. (put)

→ Chris showed me _____ _____ _____ my coat.

C 문장 완성　　우리말과 일치하도록 괄호 안의 말을 이용하여 문장을 완성하시오. (단, to부정사를 사용할 것)

1 건강을 유지하는 것은 어렵다. (it, hard, stay fit)

　→ _____

2 내 꿈은 유네스코에서 일하는 것이다. (dream, work for UNESCO)

　→ _____

3 Daniel은 나에게 쓰레기를 버리라고 말했다. (tell, take out the garbage)

　→ _____

4 나는 복권에 당첨되기를 바란다. (wish, win the lottery)

　→ _____

5 Allen은 환자들을 돌보는 것을 배웠다. (learn, care for patients)

　→ _____

6 나는 취업 면접을 위해 무엇을 입어야 할지 모르겠다. (know, wear, for the job interview)

　→ _____

D 문장 전환　　필요한 곳에 to를 넣어 문장을 다시 쓰시오.

1 It is not good drink soda very often.

　→ _____

2 I plan finish this report by this weekend.

　→ _____

3 My dream is be a professional gamer.

　→ _____

4 I want you prepare breakfast for me.

　→ _____

5 Have you decided when go to Spain?

　→ _____

6 Tim promised buy me dinner on Sunday.

　→ _____

GRAMMAR FOCUS

① **to부정사의 형용사적 용법**

to부정사가 형용사처럼 쓰여 앞에 있는 명사나 대명사를 꾸며주며, '~할, ~하는'으로 해석한다.

Do you have *any books* **to recommend**? 너는 **추천할** 책이 있니?

He had *a chance* **to visit** Paris. 그는 파리를 **방문할** 기회가 있었다.

The dog is looking for *something* **to eat**. 그 개는 **먹을** 것을 찾고 있다.

② **-thing / -body / -one + 형용사 + to부정사**

-thing, -body, -one으로 끝나는 대명사를 형용사와 to부정사가 같이 수식하는 경우에는 「대명사 + 형용사 + to부정사」의 어순으로 쓴다.

I have *something* **interesting to tell** you. 너에게 **말해 줄 흥미로운** 이야기가 있어.

She wants *someone* **creative to decorate** her house. 그녀는 자신의 집을 **꾸며 줄 창의인** 사람을 원한다.

③ **(대)명사 + to부정사 + 전치사**

to부정사가 꾸며주는 명사나 대명사가 전치사의 목적어인 경우, to부정사 뒤에 전치사를 빠뜨리지 않도록 한다.

He bought *a house* **to live in**. (← **live in** a house) 그는 **살** 집을 구입했다.

I gave my puppy *a toy* **to play with**. (← **play with** a toy) 나는 우리 강아지에게 **가지고 놀** 장난감을 주었다.

> **plus** 자주 쓰이는 「(대)명사 + to부정사 + 전치사」 표현
> - a chair **to sit on** 앉을 의자
> - something **to talk about** 이야기할 것
> - a pen **to write with** 쓸 펜
> - a friend **to play with** 함께 놀 친구
> - someone **to talk to[with]** 이야기할 사람
> - paper **to write on** 쓸 종이

EXERCISE
A 자연스러운 문장이 되도록 연결하시오.

1 He has some packages	ⓐ to drink?
2 There are many places	ⓑ to upset you.
3 I'll say nothing more	ⓒ to try new things.
4 Ann saved enough money	ⓓ to visit in Seoul.
5 Vacations give us a chance	ⓔ to do with her children.
6 Can I have something cold	ⓕ to send to his friend.
7 Oliver bought some comic books	ⓖ to read in his free time.
8 Jessica looking for something fun	ⓗ to buy a plane ticket for her trip.

EXERCISE B

〈보기〉에서 알맞은 전치사를 골라 문장을 완성하시오. (×는 필요 없음을 뜻함)

보기	at	on	with	about	×

1 You have nothing to worry _____.

2 Do you have any magazines to read _____?

3 I don't have many friends to play _____.

4 Could you bring me something to eat _____?

5 We found a bench to sit _____ by the lake.

6 Tony is looking for a partner to dance _____.

7 I booked a hotel to stay _____ during my trip.

8 They wanted some water to drink _____.

9 He handed me a sheet of paper to write _____.

10 Sue has some emails to write _____ today.

EXERCISE C

우리말과 일치하도록 빈칸에 알맞은 말을 쓰시오.

1 그녀는 요즘 체육관에 갈 시간이 없다.

→ She has no time _____ _____ to the gym these days.

2 John은 그 회사에서 일할 기회를 가졌다.

→ John had an opportunity _____ _____ at the company.

3 이 웹사이트에는 들을 만한 좋은 음악이 많이 있다.

→ This website has a lot of great music _____ _____ _____.

4 내 여동생은 가지고 놀 장난감이 많이 있다.

→ My little sister has many toys _____ _____ _____.

5 오늘 밤 TV에서 볼 흥미로운 프로그램이 있다.

→ There is something _____ _____ _____ on TV tonight.

6 그들은 그 아이들을 도울 용감한 사람이 필요하다.

→ They need someone _____ _____ _____ the children.

WRITING FOCUS

A 배열 영작   우리말과 일치하도록 괄호 안의 말을 바르게 배열하시오.

1 그 도시에는 볼거리가 많이 있다. (there, to, things, are, many, see)

→ _____ in the city.

2 너는 요즘에 운동할 시간이 있니? (you, to, time, do, have, exercise)

→ _____ these days?

3 그녀는 남편에게 줄 넥타이를 골랐다. (tie, give, a, she, to, chose)

→ _____ to her husband.

4 나는 캠핑 여행을 위해 사야 할 것들을 적었다. (to, things, I, buy, wrote down)

→ _____ for the camping trip.

5 맛있는 먹을거리를 만들자. (something, make, to, delicious, eat)

→ Let's _____ .

6 나는 내 상황에 대해 이야기할 사람이 필요하다. (I, someone, need, talk, to, with)

→ _____ about my situation.

B 빈칸 완성   우리말과 일치하도록 괄호 안의 말을 이용하여 빈칸에 알맞은 말을 쓰시오.

1 이것은 대답하기 어려운 문제이다. (question, answer)

→ This is a difficult _____ _____ _____ .

2 Ben은 그의 선생님에게 전달할 편지 한 통이 있다. (letter, deliver)

→ Ben has a _____ _____ _____ to his teacher.

3 그곳은 가을철에 등산하기에 아주 좋은 곳이다. (place, hike)

→ It is a great _____ _____ _____ during the fall season.

4 최신 유행의 입을 것이 필요하세요? (something, wear, fashionable)

→ Do you need _____ _____ _____ _____ ?

5 만일 네가 기댈 사람이 필요하면 언제든지 나에게 전화해. (someone, rely on)

→ If you need _____ _____ _____ _____ , call me anytime.

6 학생들은 이야기할 주제 하나를 고를 수 있다. (topic, talk about)

→ Students can pick a _____ _____ _____ _____ .

C 문장 완성 우리말과 일치하도록 괄호 안의 말을 이용하여 문장을 완성하시오. (단, to부정사를 사용할 것)

1 Peter는 결혼식 때 입을 양복을 샀다. (buy, a suit, wear)

→ _____ for the wedding.

2 Marie Curie는 두 개의 노벨상을 수상한 최초의 사람이었다. (the first person, win)

→ _____ two Nobel Prizes.

3 우리는 당신에게 보여 드릴 놀라운 것이 있습니다. (amazing, show you)

→ We have _____ .

4 나는 진실을 말할 충분한 용기가 없다. (enough courage, tell the truth)

→ I don't have _____ .

5 나는 앉을 의자를 찾을 수 없었다. (find, a chair, sit on)

→ I couldn't _____ .

6 고를 수 있는 두 가지 선택지가 있습니다. (option, choose from)

→ There are _____ .

D 오류 수정 어법상 틀린 부분을 바르게 고쳐 문장을 다시 쓰시오.

1 You have the right remain silent. (당신은 침묵을 지킬 권리가 있다.)

→ _____

2 I have something asking you. (당신에게 물어볼 것이 있어요.)

→ _____

3 It was a very exciting game to watching. (그것은 관람하기에 아주 흥미진진한 경기였다.)

→ _____

4 I try to find new something to experience. (나는 새로운 경험할 것을 찾으려고 노력한다.)

→ _____

5 Jean is looking for a friend to study. (Jean은 함께 공부할 친구를 찾고 있다.)

→ _____

6 They finally found the perfect house to live to. (그들은 마침내 살기에 완벽한 집을 찾았다.)

→ _____

GRAMMAR FOCUS

① to부정사의 부사적 용법

to부정사가 부사처럼 쓰여 동사, 형용사, 부사를 꾸며주며, 다양한 의미로 해석된다.

목적 (~하기 위해)	He saved money **to buy** a new car. = He saved money **in order to buy** a new car.	그는 새 차를 **사기 위해** 돈을 모았다.
감정의 원인 (~해서)	I am so glad **to meet** you.	저는 당신을 **만나서** 매우 기쁩니다.
판단의 근거 (~하다니)	She must be sad **to cry** like that.	저렇게 **울다니** 그녀는 슬픈 것이 틀림없다.
결과 (~해서 …하다)	The boy grew up **to be** an actor. I studied hard, **only to fail**. *only + to부정사: (… 했지만) 결국 ~하다	그 소년은 자라**서** 배우가 **되었다**. 나는 열심히 공부**했지만 결국 실패했다**.
형용사 수식 (~하기에)	Chinese is difficult **to learn**.	중국어는 **배우기에** 어렵다.

② too + 형용사 / 부사 + to부정사

'너무 ~해서 …할 수 없는'의 의미로, 「so + 형용사/부사 + that + 주어 + can't + 동사원형」 구문으로 바꿔 쓸 수 있다.

He is **too young to watch** that movie. 그는 너무 어려서 그 영화를 볼 수 없다.

= He is **so young that he can't watch** that movie.

Susan ran **too slowly to** win the race. Susan은 너무 느리게 달려서 그 경주에서 이길 수 없었다.

= Susan ran **so slowly that she couldn't win** the race.

③ 형용사 / 부사 + enough + to부정사

'~할 만큼 충분히 …한/하게'의 의미로, 「so + 형용사/부사 + that + 주어 + can + 동사원형」 구문으로 바꿔 쓸 수 있다.

She is **tall enough to be** a model. 그녀는 모델이 될 수 있을 만큼 충분히 키가 크다.

= She is **so tall that she can be** a model.

He studied **hard enough to pass** the exam. 그는 그 시험에 합격할 수 있을 만큼 열심히 공부했다.

= He studied **so hard that he could pass** the exam.

EXERCISE
A

다음 문장을 밑줄 친 부분에 주의하여 우리말로 해석하시오.

1 Paul went to the park <u>to walk</u> his dog.

2 I was happy <u>to receive</u> your letter.

3 I was foolish <u>to believe</u> such a thing.

4 My grandfather lived <u>to be</u> 97 years old.

5 The board game is fun <u>to play</u> with friends.

EXERCISE
B   두 문장의 의미가 같도록 빈칸에 알맞은 말을 쓰시오.

1 She is so smart that she can solve the problem.

→ She is _____ _____ _____ _____ the problem.

2 My brother is so young that he can't go to school.

→ My brother is _____ _____ _____ _____ to school.

3 I woke up so early that I could see the sunrise.

→ I woke up _____ _____ _____ _____ the sunrise.

4 The temperature is high enough to melt glass.

→ The temperature is _____ _____ _____ _____ _____

_____ glass.

5 He arrived too late to catch the train.

→ He arrived _____ _____ _____ _____

_____ the train.

EXERCISE
C   〈보기〉에서 알맞은 말을 골라 to부정사를 사용하여 문장을 완성하시오. (단, 한 번씩만 쓸 것)

보기	be	burn	borrow	complete	have
	hear	lift	swim	take	wait

1 Jake went to the library _____ some books.

2 I'm sorry _____ that your mother isn't well.

3 She grew up _____ a world-famous figure skater.

4 The old lady is too weak _____ the box.

5 The project is not easy _____ within a week.

6 He must be patient _____ for her for a long time.

7 The soup was hot enough _____ my tongue.

8 The restaurant was too noisy _____ a conversation in.

9 He bought a new camera _____ better pictures.

10 The water in the pool isn't deep enough _____ in.

WRITING FOCUS

A 배열 영작 우리말과 일치하도록 괄호 안의 말을 바르게 배열하시오.

1 Matt는 운동을 하기 위해 체육관에 갔다. (to, the, exercise, went, gym, to)

→ Matt _____ .

2 우리는 Bradford를 상대로 한 경기에 져서 실망했다. (to, the, were, lose, disappointed, we, game)

→ _____ against Bradford.

3 책상에서 잠이 들다니 그는 피곤한 것이 틀림없다. (he, tired, to, be, fall asleep, must)

→ _____ at his desk.

4 그 게임 규칙은 이해하기에 쉽지 않았다. (not, were, understand, easy, to)

→ The game rules _____ .

5 나의 학교는 너무 멀어서 집에서 걸어갈 수 없다. (too, my, walk to, far, to, is, school)

→ _____ from home.

6 날씨가 산책을 갈 수 있을 만큼 충분히 좋다. (weather, the, enough, go, fine, is, to)

→ _____ for a walk.

B 빈칸 완성 우리말과 일치하도록 괄호 안의 말을 이용하여 빈칸에 알맞은 말을 쓰시오.

1 그녀는 비행기를 타고 멕시코에 가기 위해 공항에 갔다. (fly)

→ She went to the airport _____ _____ to Mexico.

2 저는 이 세미나에 참석하게 되어 기쁩니다. (happy, attend)

→ I am _____ _____ _____ this seminar.

3 너에게 그러한 조언을 주는 것을 보니 그녀는 현명한 것이 틀림없다. (wise, give)

→ She must be _____ _____ _____ you such advice.

4 이 지갑은 너무 커서 내 주머니에 들어가지 않는다. (big, put)

→ This wallet is _____ _____ _____ _____ in my pocket.

5 날씨가 반바지를 입을 만큼 충분히 따뜻하지는 않다. (warm, wear)

→ It is not _____ _____ _____ _____ shorts.

6 그는 열심히 노력했지만 결국 운전면허 시험에서 떨어졌다. (fail, only)

→ He tried hard, _____ _____ _____ his driving test.

C 문장 완성   우리말과 일치하도록 괄호 안의 말을 이용하여 문장을 완성하시오. (단, to부정사를 사용할 것)

1 우리는 축구 경기를 보기 위해 경기장에 갔다. (watch, a soccer game)

→ We went to the stadium _____ .

2 나는 그 소식을 듣고 놀랐다. (surprised, hear)

→ _____ the news.

3 그런 말을 하다니 그는 어리석다. (stupid, say)

→ _____ such a thing.

4 그 소년은 자라서 유명한 야구 선수가 되었다. (boy, grow up, be)

→ _____ a famous baseball player.

5 Amy는 너무 바빠서 자신의 친구들과 어울려 다닐 수 없었다. (busy, hang out)

→ _____ with her friends.

6 Logan은 올림픽에 출전할 수 있을 만큼 충분히 빠르게 달린다. (run, fast, enter)

→ _____ the Olympics.

D 오류 수정   밑줄 친 부분을 바르게 고쳐 문장을 다시 쓰시오.

1 He went to the grocery store <u>for buy</u> some milk.

→ _____

2 Max must be careless <u>make</u> the same mistake again.

→ _____

3 His grandmother lived to <u>being</u> 100 years old.

→ _____

4 Your handwriting is hard <u>reading</u>.

→ _____

5 The car was <u>so big</u> to fit into the garage.

→ _____

6 The water is not <u>enough clean</u> to drink.

→ _____

to부정사의 의미상 주어와 부정

GRAMMAR FOCUS

❶ to부정사의 의미상 주어

to부정사의 행위의 주체는 to부정사 앞에 「for + 목적격」으로 나타낸다. 단, 사람의 성격이나 성품을 나타내는 형용사 뒤에는 「of + 목적격」을 쓴다.

for + 목적격	It was easy		to pass the test.	그 시험에 합격하는 것은 쉬웠다.
	It was easy	**for him**	to pass the test.	**그가** 그 시험에 합격하는 것은 쉬웠다.
of + 목적격	It is wise		to eat healthy food.	건강한 음식을 먹는 것은 현명하다.
	It is wise	**of her**	to eat healthy food.	**그녀가** 건강한 음식을 먹는 것은 현명하다.

It is helpful **for you** to learn new skills. 네가 새로운 기술을 배우는 것은 도움이 된다.

It is nice **of John** to help his friends. John이 그의 친구들을 돕는 것은 친절하다.

cf. 「of + 목적격」을 쓰는 형용사

kind / nice / sweet(친절한, 상냥한), thoughtful(사려 깊은, 친절한), generous(너그러운), wise(현명한), brave(용감한), polite(공손한), rude(무례한), careless(부주의한), foolish / silly / stupid(어리석은) 등

❷ to부정사의 부정

to부정사의 부정은 to부정사 앞에 not을 붙인다.

It is safer **not to talk** to strangers. 낯선 사람들과는 **이야기하지 않는 것이** 더 안전하다.

My family decided **not to move** to Australia. 우리 가족은 호주로 **이주하지 않기로** 결정했다.

Be careful **not to break** the glass. 그 유리잔을 **깨지 않도록** 조심해라.

괄호 안에서 알맞은 것을 고르시오.

1 It is impossible (for us, of us) to finish the work today.

2 They agreed (to not tell, not to tell) the secret to their friends.

3 The tea was too hot (for her, of her) to drink.

4 It was very exciting (for me, of me) to travel to a new country.

5 Tony decided (not to play, to not play) computer games too often.

6 This suitcase is too heavy (for Julia, of Julia) to carry.

7 It was so nice (for him, of him) to give me the flowers.

8 It was careless (for her, of her) to leave the door open.

9 This book is difficult (for me, for I) to read.

10 It is brave (for him, of him) to sing in front of the crowd.

11 I promised (to not forget, not to forget) my sister's birthday again.

EXERCISE **B**

밑줄 친 부분을 어법에 맞게 고치시오.

1 It is easy <u>of me</u> to bake cookies.

2 It is impossible <u>for we</u> to live without water.

3 This backpack is too fancy <u>for my</u> to carry.

4 It was nice <u>for him</u> to do me a favor yesterday.

5 He decided <u>to not call</u> her anymore.

6 It was polite <u>for her</u> to offer her seat to the old man.

7 This music is too slow <u>to us</u> to dance to.

8 It was very kind <u>for you</u> to help me.

9 It is hard <u>of kids</u> to stay focused on one activity.

10 It was foolish <u>of he</u> to spend all his money.

11 My mom told me <u>to not stay</u> up too late.

12 It was generous <u>to them</u> to share their food.

EXERCISE **C**

우리말과 일치하도록 빈칸에 알맞은 말을 쓰시오.

1 나는 자전거 타는 법을 배우는 것이 재미있었다.

→ It was fun _____ _____ to learn how to ride a bike.

2 그녀가 작별 인사도 하지 않고 떠난 것은 무례했다.

→ It was rude _____ _____ to leave without saying goodbye.

3 우리는 올해 휴가를 가지 않기로 결정했다.

→ We decided _____ _____ _____ on vacation this year.

4 그가 나를 공항까지 태워다 준 것은 친절했다.

→ It was kind _____ _____ to drive me to the airport.

5 그 공원에는 우리가 앉을 수 있는 멋진 잔디밭이 있다.

→ There is some nice grass _____ _____ to sit on at the park.

6 교장 선생님께서는 우리에게 복도에서 뛰지 말라고 말씀하셨다.

→ The principal told us _____ _____ _____ in the hallway.

WRITING FOCUS

A 배열 영작   우리말과 일치하도록 괄호 안의 말을 바르게 배열하시오.

1 그녀가 화를 내는 것은 당연하다. (for, natural, to, her, get angry)

→ It is _____.

2 그는 그 퍼즐을 그렇게 빨리 풀다니 영리하다. (him, the, of, puzzle, to, so, clever, solve, quickly)

→ It is _____.

3 그가 사람들의 이름을 기억하는 것은 쉽다. (easy, people's names, to, him, for, remember)

→ It is _____.

4 Nancy가 그녀의 할머니를 도와드리는 것은 착하다. (to, Nancy, her, of, nice, help, grandma)

→ It is _____.

5 나의 부모님은 나에게 거짓말을 하지 말라고 말씀하신다. (to, tell, not, lies)

→ My parents tell me _____.

6 감기에 걸리지 않도록 조심해라. (catch, a, to, cold, not)

→ Be careful _____.

B 빈칸 완성   우리말과 일치하도록 괄호 안의 말을 이용하여 빈칸에 알맞은 말을 쓰시오.

1 그녀가 그렇게 빠르게 운전한 것은 어리석었다. (drive)

→ It was stupid _____ _____ _____ _____ so fast.

2 내가 그녀의 조언을 따른 것은 실수였다. (follow)

→ It was a mistake _____ _____ _____ _____ her advice.

3 당신이 미래를 위한 계획을 세우는 것은 현명하다. (plan)

→ It is wise _____ _____ _____ _____ for your future.

4 그가 그 회의에 참석하는 것은 중요하다. (attend)

→ It is important _____ _____ _____ _____ the meeting.

5 Karen은 그 손님에게 안에서 흡연하지 말라고 말했다. (smoke)

→ Karen told the customer _____ _____ _____ inside.

6 밤 늦게 먹지 않는 것이 당신의 건강에 좋다. (eat)

→ It is good for your health _____ _____ _____ late at night.

C 문장 완성   우리말과 일치하도록 괄호 안의 말을 이용하여 문장을 완성하시오. (단, to부정사를 사용할 것)

1 그녀는 음식을 삼키는 것이 힘들었다. (difficult, swallow, food)

→ It was _____.

2 당신이 파티에 나를 초대해 준 것은 사려깊다. (thoughtful, invite, to the party)

→ It is _____.

3 우리가 충분한 물을 마시는 것이 중요하다. (important, drink, enough water)

→ It is _____.

4 네가 네 장갑을 잃어버린 것은 부주의했다. (careless, lose, gloves)

→ It was _____.

5 우리는 첫 기차를 놓치지 않으려고 집에서 일찍 출발했다. (miss, the first train)

→ We left home early _____.

6 나는 울지 않으려고 무척 애썼다. (cry)

→ I tried hard _____.

D 오류 수정   어법상 틀린 부분을 바르게 고쳐 문장을 다시 쓰시오.

1 It was kind for him to carry the bag for me. (그가 나를 위해 가방을 들어 준 것은 친절했다.)

→ _____

2 It is boring of me to watch golf on TV. (나는 TV로 골프를 보는 것이 지루하다.)

→ _____

3 It is wise for you not to make the same mistake. (네가 같은 실수를 하지 않는 것은 현명하다.)

→ _____

4 It can be helpful for we to make a to-do list. (우리가 할 일 목록을 만드는 것은 도움이 될 수 있다.)

→ _____

5 We hurried to not be late for the meeting. (우리는 그 회의에 늦지 않기 위해 서둘렀다.)

→ _____

6 My parents decided not go to Europe in July. (나의 부모님은 7월에 유럽을 가지 않기로 결정하셨다.)

→ _____

01 밑줄 친 It의 쓰임이 나머지 넷과 다른 것은?

① It is hot and humid today.

② It is difficult to write a novel.

③ It is fun to play with your friends.

④ It is important to be kind to others.

⑤ It is hard for him to run a marathon.

02 밑줄 친 부분이 틀린 것은?

① He forgot where to meet her.

② Can you show me how to cook rice?

③ I don't know why to choose this color.

④ I've decided what to wear to the party.

⑤ I asked him when to take the medicine.

빈출
03 〈보기〉의 밑줄 친 부분과 쓰임이 같은 것은?

보기 He has a dream to become a singer.

① We need to recycle plastic waste.

② I'm sorry to call you so late at night.

③ My dream is to speak English fluently.

④ He is studying hard to get good grades.

⑤ There are many interesting books to read.

04 밑줄 친 부분이 어법상 올바른 것은?

① There is no chair to sit.

② She wants someone to talk.

③ I need some paper to write in.

④ They bought a new house to live to.

⑤ He doesn't have a spoon to eat with.

05 밑줄 친 to를 in order to로 바꿔 쓸 수 있는 것은?

① Is Chinese difficult to learn?

② Mary did her best, only to fail.

③ I went shopping to buy new clothes.

④ They were surprised to hear the news.

⑤ He must be very smart to graduate early.

06 주어진 문장과 의미가 같도록 바르게 바꾼 것은?

I am too tired to go to the gym.

① I am so tired to go to the gym.

② I am so tired that I can't go to the gym.

③ I am too tired that I can't go to the gym.

④ I am tired enough that I can go to the gym.

⑤ I am enough tired that I can't go to the gym.

07 빈칸에 들어갈 말이 순서대로 짝지어진 것은?

• It is rude _____ him to act like that.

• This book is easy _____ me to read.

① of – to   ② for – of

③ of – for   ④ for – to

⑤ to – for

고난도

08 어법상 올바른 문장을 <u>모두</u> 고르면?

ⓐ To laugh is good for your health.
ⓑ There is to eat something in the fridge.
ⓒ We hurried not to be late for the concert.
ⓓ He saved money in order to buy a house.
ⓔ The mountain is too steep for we to climb.
ⓕ She is enough tall to ride the roller coaster.

① ⓐ, ⓓ, ⓔ　　　　② ⓐ, ⓒ, ⓓ
③ ⓑ, ⓒ　　　　　④ ⓒ, ⓓ, ⓔ
⑤ ⓓ, ⓔ, ⓕ

✏ 서술형

09 우리말과 일치하도록 주어진 말을 바르게 배열하시오.

(1) 아침 식사를 거르는 것은 건강에 좋지 않다.
(is, breakfast, to, unhealthy, it, skip)

→ _____

(2) 우리는 그 영화를 보지 않기로 결정했다.
(decided, we, watch, not, the, to, movie)

→ _____

10 우리말과 일치하도록 〈보기〉에서 필요한 단어들만 골라 배열하여 문장을 완성하시오.

우리는 저녁 식사로 무엇을 주문할 지에 대해 이야기했다.

보기	talked	how	to	for dinner
	order	we	about	what

→ _____

11 주어진 문장과 의미가 같도록 빈칸에 알맞은 말을 쓰시오.

I don't know where to put this lamp.

→ I don't know _____ _____

_____ _____ this lamp.

12 우리말과 일치하도록 주어진 말을 활용하여 문장을 완성하시오.

(1) 그녀는 그것을 살 돈이 없다. (money, no, buy, it)

→ She has _____ .

(2) 그는 자신의 약속을 어길 사람이 아니다.
(a person, break, promise)

→ He is not _____ .

13 밑줄 친 부분을 어법에 맞게 고치시오.

(1) It is good to <u>getting</u> enough sleep.
(충분한 수면을 취하는 것이 좋다.)

→ _____

(2) His accent was <u>to understand difficult</u>.
(그의 억양은 이해하기 어려웠다.)

→ _____

14 빈칸에 들어갈 말을 〈보기〉에서 골라 알맞은 형태로 쓰시오.

보기	borrow	find	see

(1) He was shocked _____ the accident.

(2) I went to the library _____ a book.

(3) She entered the room _____ it empty.

15 그림을 보고, 〈조건〉에 맞게 문장을 완성하시오.

> 조건 1. 가주어 it 을 사용할 것
> 2. dangerous, use, your smartphone을 사용할 것

→ _____ _____ _____

_____ _____ _____

_____ when you cross the street.

16 우리말과 일치하도록 주어진 말을 활용하여 문장을 완성하시오.

그녀는 나에게 뜨거운 마실 것을 가져다주었다.
(something, drink, hot)

→ She brought me _____ .

17 주어진 문장과 의미가 같도록 to부정사를 사용하여 문장을 바꿔 쓰시오.

(1) I was so busy that I couldn't call you yesterday.

→ _____

(2) The robot is so strong that it can lift the heavy box.

→ _____

18 어법상 틀린 문장 2개를 골라 기호를 쓰고, 틀린 부분을 바르게 고치시오.

> ⓐ I hope to write a book someday.
> ⓑ They didn't know where they to park.
> ⓒ He edited photos to post on his blog.
> ⓓ To achieve success, you must set clear goals.
> ⓔ It is so nice for him to buy me a gift.
> ⓕ The important thing is not to give up.

(   ) _____ → _____

(   ) _____ → _____

19 우리말과 일치하도록 〈조건〉에 맞게 문장을 완성하시오.

> 조건 1. 괄호 안의 말과 to부정사의 의미상 주어를 사용할 것
> 2. (1)과 (2) 각각 총 8단어로 쓸 것

(1) 내가 그를 설득하는 것은 불가능하다.
(impossible, it, persuade)

→ _____

(2) 그가 우리를 도와준 것은 친절했다. (kind, it, help)

→ _____

20 어법상 틀린 것을 찾아 기호를 쓰고 바르게 고치시오.

> A: I'm planning ⓐto go on a camping trip next week, but I'm not sure ⓑwhat to prepare.
> B: ⓒIt might help to write everything down on paper.
> A: That's a great idea! I'll bring a pen ⓓto write.

(   ) → _____

Chapter 05

동명사

동명사는 「동사원형 + -ing」 형태이며, 문장에서 명사처럼 쓰인다. 동명사는 동사의 성질도 있기 때문에 뒤에 목적어를 취할 수 있다.

❶ 동명사의 역할

동명사는 명사처럼 쓰여 문장에서 주어, 보어, 목적어 역할을 하며, '~하는 것, ~하기'로 해석한다.

주어	**Watching** a movie *is* a lot of fun. ＊주어 자리에 쓰인 동명사(구)는 단수 취급	영화를 **보는 것은** 매우 재미있다.
보어	One of my hobbies is **dancing**.	내 취미 중 하나는 **춤추는 것이다.**
동사의 목적어	Tiffany *enjoyed* **staying** in Chicago.	Tiffany는 시카고에 **머무는 것을** 즐겼다.
전치사의 목적어	Sally is interested *in* **joining** a choir.	Sally는 합창단에 **가입하는 것에** 관심이 있다.

> **plus** 동명사 vs. 진행형
>
> 동명사는 be동사 뒤에서 보어로 쓰여 '~하는 것(이다)'의 의미를, 진행형은 '~하고 있다'의 의미를 나타낸다.
>
> His job **is repairing** cars. 그의 직업은 자동차를 **수리하는 것이다.** 〈동명사〉
>
> He **is repairing** a car. 그는 자동차를 **수리하고 있다.** 〈진행형〉

❷ 자주 쓰이는 동명사 구문

· go v-ing	~하러 가다	· have difficulty v-ing	~하는 데 어려움을 겪다
· be busy v-ing	~하느라 바쁘다	· spend + 시간/돈 + v-ing	~하는 데 시간/돈을 쓰다
· be worth v-ing	~할 가치가 있다	· It is no use v-ing	~해도 소용없다
· How[What] about v-ing ~?	~하는 게 어때?	· cannot help v-ing	~하지 않을 수 없다
· feel like v-ing	~하고 싶다	· look forward to v-ing	~하기를 고대하다

I **went skiing** last weekend. 나는 지난 주말에 **스키를 타러 갔다.**

Sam **is busy doing** his homework. Sam은 그의 숙제를 **하느라 바쁘다.**

I **had difficulty understanding** his explanation. 나는 그의 설명을 **이해하는 데 어려움을 겪었다.**

Lily **spent too much money buying** clothes. Lily는 옷을 **사는 데 너무 많은 돈을 썼다.**

It is no use crying over spilt milk. 우유를 엎지르고 **울어도 소용없다.** (이미 엎질러진 물이다.)

He **couldn't help smiling** at her words. 그는 그녀의 말에 **미소 짓지 않을 수 없었다.**

We **look forward to seeing** you again. 우리는 당신을 다시 **뵙기를 고대합니다.**

EXERCISE A

밑줄 친 동명사가 문장에서 주어, 보어, 목적어 중 어떤 역할을 하는지 쓰시오.

1 My new hobby is <u>playing</u> badminton.

2 <u>Reading</u> good books is important.

3 Would you mind <u>turning</u> off the light?

4 Andrew's job is <u>teaching</u> English to children.

5 Thank you for <u>inviting</u> me to your birthday party.

EXERCISE B

〈보기〉에서 알맞은 말을 골라 동명사 형태로 바꿔 문장을 완성하시오.

보기	join	say	clean	eat

1 _____ a club is a good way to make friends.

2 He kept _____ sweets to stay awake.

3 My brother hates _____ his room.

4 She left the room without _____ a word.

EXERCISE C

다음 문장을 밑줄 친 부분에 주의하여 우리말로 해석하시오.

1 I <u>was busy preparing</u> a meal.

→ _____

2 I don't <u>feel like going</u> to school today.

→ _____

3 This museum <u>is worth visiting</u>.

→ _____

4 <u>It is no use asking</u> him for help.

→ _____

5 I am <u>looking forward to hearing</u> from you soon.

→ _____

WRITING FOCUS

A 배열 영작   우리말과 일치하도록 괄호 안의 말을 바르게 배열하시오.

1 규칙적으로 식사하는 것은 당신의 건강에 좋다. (regularly, for, good, eating, your, is, health)

  ➡ _____

2 내 취미 중 하나는 빵을 굽는 것이다. (my, of, baking, hobbies, is, bread, one)

  ➡ _____

3 Emily는 다른 도시로 이사 가는 것을 고려하고 있다. (considering, Emily, is, to, moving, another city)

  ➡ _____

4 그는 장학금을 받은 것을 자랑스러워한다. (a, he, scholarship, is, getting, proud of)

  ➡ _____

5 그 작문 수업은 들을 만한 가치가 있었다. (writing class, was, the, taking, worth)

  ➡ _____

6 그녀는 도서관 카드를 발급받는 데 어려움을 겪었다. (had, a, getting, she, difficulty, library card)

  ➡ _____

B 빈칸 완성   우리말과 일치하도록 괄호 안의 말을 이용하여 빈칸에 알맞은 말을 쓰시오.

1 아이들을 키우는 것은 돈이 많이 든다. (raise, children)

  ➡ _____ _____ costs a lot of money.

2 그는 운동으로 수영하는 것을 즐긴다. (enjoy, swim)

  ➡ He _____ _____ for exercise.

3 Linda의 취미는 오래된 장난감들을 수집하는 것이다. (collect)

  ➡ Linda's hobby _____ _____ old toys.

4 Joseph은 지난주에 그의 아버지와 낚시를 하러 갔다. (go, fish)

  ➡ Joseph _____ _____ with his father last week.

5 그 아이들은 커다란 눈사람을 만드느라 바빴다. (busy, make)

  ➡ The children _____ _____ _____ a big snowman.

6 그는 자신의 연구를 포기하지 않을 수 없었다. (help, give up)

  ➡ He _____ _____ _____ _____ his research.

C 문장 완성   우리말과 일치하도록 괄호 안의 말을 이용하여 문장을 완성하시오. (단, 동명사를 사용할 것)

1 그의 일은 택배를 배달하는 것이다. (job, deliver, packages)

→ _____

2 그는 클래식 음악 듣는 것을 즐긴다. (enjoy, listen to, classical music)

→ _____

3 스페인어 수업을 듣는 것은 재미있다. (take, a Spanish class, interesting)

→ _____

4 Cindy는 TV를 보는 데 많은 시간을 보냈다. (spend, a lot of, watch TV)

→ _____

5 그가 안쓰럽다고 해도 소용없다. (it, use, feel sorry for)

→ _____

6 Bill은 통화하느라 바빴다. (busy, talk on the phone)

→ _____

D 오류 수정   어법상 틀린 부분을 바르게 고쳐 문장을 다시 쓰시오.

1 Breaking bad habits are not easy. (나쁜 습관을 고치는 것은 쉽지 않다.)

→ _____

2 My brother is worried about join the army. (나의 형은 입대하는 것을 걱정한다.)

→ _____

3 What about write a thank-you letter to her? (그녀에게 감사 편지를 쓰는 게 어때?)

→ _____

4 She spends a lot of time to practice the piano. (그녀는 피아노를 연습하는 데 많은 시간을 보낸다.)

→ _____

5 He is having difficulty to finding a job. (그는 일자리를 찾는 데 어려움을 겪고 있다.)

→ _____

6 She is looking forward to visit her family. (그녀는 자신의 가족을 방문하는 것을 고대하고 있다.)

→ _____

02 동명사 vs. to부정사

GRAMMAR FOCUS

① 동명사를 목적어로 취하는 동사

enjoy	keep	stop	avoid	practice	postpone
mind	finish	quit	give up	consider	put off

She *enjoys* **drinking** tea in the afternoon. 그녀는 오후에 차 마시는 것을 즐긴다.

Jim *finished* **doing** his homework. Jim은 그의 숙제하는 것을 끝냈다.

② to부정사를 목적어로 취하는 동사

want	hope	plan	decide	wish	agree
need	expect	promise	learn	fail	refuse

They *want* **to move** to a bigger house. 그들은 더 큰 집으로 이사하고 싶어한다.

Jenny *decided* **to grow** her hair. Jenny는 머리를 기르기로 결심했다.

③ 동명사와 to부정사를 모두 목적어로 취하는 동사

둘 다 목적어로 취하는 동사	like, love, hate, dislike, start, begin, continue 등	
둘 다 목적어로 취하되 의미가 달라지는 동사	remember v-ing ～한 것을 기억하다	remember to-v ～할 것을 기억하다
	forget v-ing ～한 것을 잊다	forget to-v ～할 것을 잊다
	try v-ing (시험 삼아) ～해 보다	try to-v ～하려고 노력하다

He *likes* **playing**[**to play**] the guitar. 그는 기타 연주하는 것을 좋아한다.

I *remember* **calling** my friend. 나는 내 친구에게 전화한 것을 기억한다.

I *remember* **to call** my friend. 나는 내 친구에게 전화해야 할 것을 기억한다.

cf. 「stop + to부정사」에 쓰인 to부정사는 부사적 용법으로 목적(～하기 위해)을 나타낸다.

They *stopped* **discussing** the matter. 그들은 그 문제를 **논의하는 것을** 멈추었다.

They *stopped* **to discuss** the matter. 그들은 그 문제를 **논의하기 위해** (하던 일을) 멈추었다.

EXERCISE A

괄호 안에서 알맞은 것을 <u>모두</u> 고르시오.

1 She promised (calling, to call) me later.

2 He finished (writing, to write) his report just in time.

3 I need (buying, to buy) a new pair of shoes.

4 My father quit (smoking, to smoke) two years ago.

5 She loves (walking, to walk) in the park.

6 I started (learning, to learn) a new language online.

EXERCISE

B

괄호 안의 말을 알맞은 형태로 바꿔 문장을 완성하시오.

1 Helen planned _____ her friend a party. (throw)

2 The students enjoyed _____ various games. (play)

3 She avoids _____ food late at night. (eat)

4 My school football team failed _____ the game. (win)

5 He doesn't mind _____ to work in the morning. (walk)

6 Ethan gave up _____ the old bicycle. (fix)

7 The club members agreed _____ once a month. (meet)

8 They put off _____ the laundry until the weekend. (do)

9 She will learn _____ before summer. (swim)

10 We practice _____ English every day. (speak)

11 They kept _____ about their favorite TV show. (talk)

12 Sally and Jane expect _____ next year. (graduate)

EXERCISE

C

괄호 안의 말을 이용하여 문장을 완성하시오.

1 너는 나와 함께 영화관에 갔던 것을 기억하니? (go)

→ Do you remember _____ to the theater with me?

2 아침에 약 먹는 것을 잊지 마세요. (take)

→ Don't forget _____ the medicine in the morning.

3 그는 그 피아노를 옮기려고 애를 썼다. (move)

→ He tried _____ the piano.

4 전원 버튼을 10초 동안 눌러 보세요. (press)

→ Try _____ the power button for 10 seconds.

5 비는 한 시간 뒤에 그쳤다. (rain)

→ It stopped _____ after an hour.

6 그 소년은 동전을 줍기 위해 멈춰 섰다. (pick up)

→ The boy stopped _____ the coin.

WRITING FOCUS

A 배열 영작　우리말과 일치하도록 괄호 안의 말을 바르게 배열하시오. (단, 필요시 형태를 바꿀 것)

1 창문을 열어도 될까요? (mind, window, you, do, the, open)

→ _____

2 우리는 곧 당신을 뵙기를 희망합니다. (see, we, you, hope, soon)

→ _____

3 나는 그곳에 갔던 것이 기억나지 않는다. (I, go, remember, don't, there)

→ _____

4 나는 내 휴대폰 충전하는 것을 잊어버렸다. (cellphone, forgot, my, I, charge)

→ _____

5 그녀는 처음으로 회를 먹어 보았다. (tried, raw fish, she, eat, for the first time)

→ _____

6 그는 그 병의 뚜껑을 열려고 애를 썼다. (tried, the lid, he, open, of the jar)

→ _____

B 빈칸 완성　우리말과 일치하도록 괄호 안의 말을 이용하여 빈칸에 알맞은 말을 쓰시오.

1 우리는 매일 저녁 크리스마스 캐럴 부르는 것을 연습했다. (practice, sing)

→ We _____ _____ carols every evening.

2 너는 졸업 후에 외국에서 공부할 계획이니? (plan, study)

→ Do you _____ _____ _____ abroad after graduation?

3 밤에는 강 근처에 가는 것을 피하세요. (avoid, go)

→ Please _____ _____ near the river at night.

4 Matthew는 언젠가 소설을 쓰고 싶어한다. (wish, write)

→ Matthew _____ _____ _____ a novel someday.

5 나는 오늘 내 친구에게 전화해야 할 것을 기억한다. (remember, call)

→ I _____ _____ _____ my friend today.

6 그녀는 그 교량의 사진을 찍기 위해 멈춰 섰다. (stop, take)

→ She _____ _____ _____ a picture of the bridge.

C 문장 완성 우리말과 일치하도록 괄호 안의 말을 이용하여 문장을 완성하시오.

1 나는 학교 합창단에 가입하는 것을 고려 중이다. (consider, join the school choir)

➡ _____

2 그녀는 진실을 말하기로 약속했다. (promise, tell the truth)

➡ _____

3 그는 컴퓨터 게임하는 것을 그만두었다. (stop, play computer games)

➡ _____

4 너는 네 나쁜 습관을 바꿀 필요가 있다. (need, change, bad habits)

➡ _____

5 우리는 비 오는 날에는 영화 보는 것을 즐긴다. (enjoy, watch movies, on rainy days)

➡ _____

6 그들은 그 보호소에서 개 한 마리를 입양하기로 결정했다. (decide, adopt a dog, from the shelter)

➡ _____

D 오류 수정 밑줄 친 부분을 바르게 고쳐 문장을 다시 쓰시오.

1 She wants take up a new hobby. (그녀는 새로운 취미를 갖고 싶어한다.)

➡ _____

2 They finished pack their bags for the trip. (그들은 여행을 위해 짐 싸는 것을 마쳤다.)

➡ _____

3 We should learn live with other people. (우리는 다른 사람들과 함께 사는 것을 배워야 한다.)

➡ _____

4 I will keep exercise to stay healthy. (나는 건강을 유지하기 위해 운동을 계속할 것이다.)

➡ _____

5 Kate failed pass the driving test again. (Kate는 또다시 운전면허 시험에 합격하지 못했다.)

➡ _____

6 Don't forget feed the cat before you go out. (나가기 전에 고양이에게 먹이 주는 것을 잊지 마.)

➡ _____

01 빈칸에 들어갈 말로 알맞은 것은?

> She decided _____ at the local charity.

① volunteer
② volunteers
③ volunteered
④ to volunteer
⑤ volunteering

02 빈칸에 들어갈 말로 알맞지 <u>않은</u> 것은?

> _____ swimming early in the morning.

① Ben likes
② Sue learns
③ Mark enjoys
④ Andy gave up
⑤ Lisa doesn't mind

빈출

03 밑줄 친 부분의 쓰임이 나머지 넷과 <u>다른</u> 것은?

① Thank you for <u>coming</u>.
② Is Mike <u>studying</u> in his room?
③ <u>Cooking</u> is my favorite activity.
④ Her bad habit is <u>biting</u> her fingernails.
⑤ We practiced <u>passing</u> the ball to each other.

04 밑줄 친 부분을 동명사로 바꿔 쓸 수 <u>없는</u> 것은?

① I hate <u>to go</u> to crowded places.
② Sue loves <u>to shop</u> on the Internet.
③ He promised <u>to call</u> me later today.
④ Tom started <u>to learn</u> a new language.
⑤ They continued <u>to jump</u> on the trampoline.

05 우리말을 영어로 바르게 옮긴 것은?

> 우산 가져가는 것을 잊지 마라.

① Don't forget bring an umbrella.
② Don't forget to bring an umbrella.
③ Don't forget bringing an umbrella.
④ Don't forget to brought an umbrella.
⑤ Don't forget to bringing an umbrella.

06 대화의 빈칸에 들어갈 말이 순서대로 짝지어진 것은?

> A: Emily, what club are you going to join?
> B: I want _____ the gardening club.
>   I'm interested in _____ plants and flowers.

① join – grow
② to join – to grow
③ to join – growing
④ joining – to grow
⑤ joining – growing

07 괄호 안의 동사를 알맞은 형태로 바꿀 때, 동명사 형태로 써야 하는 문장의 개수는?

ⓐ Sam failed (persuade) his father.
ⓑ He often puts off (do) his homework.
ⓒ Let's go (fish) in the river this weekend.
ⓓ My sister hopes (major) in art in college.
ⓔ My laptop keeps (turn) off unexpectedly.
ⓕ I will finish (write) the report by 8 o'clock.

① 2개
② 3개
③ 4개
④ 4개
⑤ 6개

고난도

08 어법상 올바른 문장을 <u>모두</u> 고르면?

    ⓐ I feel like eating pizza for lunch.
    ⓑ Do you mind to wait for a moment?
    ⓒ Remember taking your medicine daily.
    ⓓ She is proud of winning the competition.
    ⓔ Making a big decision take time and energy.

① ⓐ, ⓑ   ② ⓐ, ⓓ
③ ⓐ, ⓓ, ⓔ   ④ ⓑ, ⓒ, ⓔ
⑤ ⓓ, ⓔ

🖋 서술형

09 주어진 말을 활용하여 문장을 완성하시오.

(1) She enjoys _____ selfies. (take)

(2) We need _____ groceries for the week. (buy)

(3) I'm sorry for _____ late. (be)

10 어법상 <u>틀린</u> 부분을 찾아 〈조건〉에 맞게 고쳐 문장을 다시 쓰시오.

> **조건** 단어의 수를 바꾸지 말 것

(1) Her hobby is play the violin.

→ _____

(2) Make friends is not always easy.

→ _____

11 우리말과 일치하도록 주어진 말을 바르게 배열하시오. (단, 필요시 형태를 바꿀 것)

(1) 그는 저녁 8시 이후에 먹는 것을 피한다.
    (avoids, eat, he, after 8:00 p.m.)

→ _____

(2) 나는 발표하는 것이 걱정된다.
    (I, presentation, worried, a, give, am, about)

→ _____

12 우리말과 일치하도록 〈조건〉에 맞게 문장을 완성하시오.

> **조건** 괄호 안의 말과 stop을 활용할 것

(1) 그녀는 자신의 신발 끈을 묶기 위해 멈춰 섰다. (tie)

→ She _____ her shoelaces.

(2) 우리는 환경을 위해 비닐봉지 사용하는 것을 멈춰야 한다. (use)

→ We should _____ plastic bags for the environment.

13 두 문장을 한 문장으로 바꿔 쓸 때, 빈칸에 알맞은 말을 쓰시오.

(1) I saw Sophia at the party. I remember it.

→ I remember _____ Sophia at the party.

(2) Jack didn't lock the door. He forgot it.

→ Jack forgot _____ the door.

14 빈칸에 들어갈 말을 〈보기〉에서 골라 알맞은 형태로 쓰시오. (중복 사용 가능)

> **보기**   ask   bake

A: I want (1) _____ a cake, but I don't know what to do.
B: How about (2) _____ Tara? She is good at (3) _____ delicious cakes.

15 그림을 보고, 주어진 말을 활용하여 문장을 완성하시오.

→ Emily _____ _____
_____ _____ last night.
(difficulty, fall asleep)

고난도

18 밑줄 친 우리말과 일치하도록 〈조건〉에 맞게 문장을 완성하시오.

A: (1) 졸업 후에 무엇을 할 계획이니? (plan, do)

B: (2) 어학 실력을 향상시키기 위해 유학을 고려하고 있어. (consider, study abroad)

조건 1. 괄호 안에 주어진 말을 활용할 것
2. (1)은 6단어, (2)는 5단어를 추가하여 문장을 완성할 것
3. 현재진행형을 사용할 것

(1) _____
after graduation?

(2) _____
to improve my language skills.

16 우리말과 일치하도록 주어진 말을 바르게 배열하시오.

(1) 과거에 대해 불평해도 소용없다.

(use, it, the, no, about, complaining, is, past)

→ _____

(2) 나는 그의 농담에 웃지 않을 수 없었다.

(his, help, at, I, laughing, couldn't, jokes)

→ _____

[19~20] 다음 글을 읽고, 물음에 답하시오.

Dear Paul,

How is your vacation going? I'm spending time to play with my friends. I'm also trying to do various activities like hiking and swimming. How about you? Are you still busy preparing for the big exam? I really want to meet you and have some fun. 너를 곧 보기를 고대하고 있어. (forward, see)

Harry

고난도

19 어법상 틀린 문장을 찾아 바르게 고치시오.

→ _____

17 우리말과 일치하도록 주어진 말을 활용하여 문장을 완성하시오.

(1) 그 책은 두 번 읽을 가치가 있다. (worth, read)

→ The book _____ twice.

(2) 그는 종종 공원에 조깅을 하러 간다. (go, jog)

→ He often _____ in the park.

20 밑줄 친 우리말과 일치하도록 주어진 말을 활용하여 문장을 완성하시오.

→ I am _____ _____
_____ you soon.

Chapter 06

분사

현재분사와 과거분사

❶ 분사의 개념과 종류

동사에 -ing 또는 -ed를 붙여 형용사처럼 사용하는 것으로 현재분사와 과거분사가 있다.

현재분사	동사원형 + **-ing**	능동(~하는) 진행(~하고 있는)	**surprising** news **falling** leaves	놀라운 소식 떨어지는 나뭇잎들
과거분사	동사원형 + **-ed**, 불규칙 과거분사	수동(~된) 완료(~한)	**surprised** people **fallen** leaves	놀란 사람들 떨어진 나뭇잎들

The **smiling** boy waved at us. 그 **웃고 있는** 소년은 우리에게 손을 흔들었다.

They walked across the **frozen** lake. 그들은 **얼어붙은** 호수 위를 걸어갔다.

❷ 분사의 쓰임

(1) 명사 수식: 분사가 명사를 단독으로 수식할 때는 주로 명사 앞에 오며, 다른 어구와 함께 쓰여 길어질 때는 명사 뒤에서 수식한다.

Look at the **flying** birds. 날아가는 새들을 봐.

He bought a car **made** in Germany. 그는 독일에서 만들어진 차를 한 대 샀다.

(2) 보어 역할: 분사는 주격보어와 목적격보어로 쓰일 수 있다.

I felt **bored** with my work. 나는 내 일에 지루함을 느꼈다. 〈주격보어〉

We saw a man **singing** in the park. 우리는 한 남자가 공원에서 노래하고 있는 것을 보았다. 〈목적격보어〉

plus 현재분사와 동명사는 둘 다 「동사원형 + -ing」 형태이지만 쓰임이 다르므로 주의해야 한다.

	현재분사	동명사
명사 앞	a **sleeping** baby 잠자고 있는 아기 〈명사 수식〉	a **sleeping** pill 잠을 위한 약 → 수면제 〈명사의 용도 설명〉
be동사 뒤	He is **teaching** English. 그는 영어를 가르치고 있다. 〈진행형〉	His job is **teaching** English. 그의 직업은 영어를 가르치는 것이다. 〈주격보어〉

EXERCISE A

괄호 안에서 알맞은 말을 고르시오.

1 The (crying, cried) baby finally fell asleep.

2 Try this freshly (baking, baked) bread.

3 The dog (wagging, wagged) its tail is cute.

4 He changed the (breaking, broken) windows.

5 I raked (falling, fallen) leaves in the garden.

6 We saw the kids (playing, played) tag in the park.

EXERCISE B

다음 문장을 밑줄 친 부분에 주의하여 우리말로 해석하시오.

1 The <u>swimming</u> children are wearing life jackets.

→ _____

2 The police found the <u>stolen</u> car.

→ _____

3 The boy <u>running</u> over there is my little brother.

→ _____

4 There was some food <u>left</u> on the plate.

→ _____

5 The necklace <u>made</u> of gold is very expensive.

→ _____

6 Do you know the girl <u>talking</u> to John?

→ _____

EXERCISE C

우리말과 일치하도록 〈보기〉에서 알맞은 동사를 골라 분사 형태로 바꿔 문장을 완성하시오.

보기	play	write	read	name	enter

1 나에게는 Mini라는 이름의 고양이 한 마리가 있다.

→ I have a cat _____ Mini.

2 저기 책을 읽고 있는 소년을 봐.

→ Look at the boy _____ a book over there.

3 거실에서 놀고 있는 아이들은 내 사촌이다.

→ The kids _____ in the living room are my cousins.

4 영어로 쓰여진 책은 읽기가 어렵다.

→ Books _____ in English are hard to read.

5 Jack은 그의 친구들이 그 건물에 들어가고 있는 것을 보았다.

→ Jack saw his friends _____ the building.

WRITING FOCUS

A 배열 영작   우리말과 일치하도록 괄호 안의 말을 바르게 배열하시오.

1 우리는 낙엽 위를 걸었다. (walked, we, leaves, on, fallen)

→ _____

2 흐르는 물에 손을 씻으세요. (wash, your, running, under, hands, water)

→ _____

3 이것들은 Andy가 찍은 사진이다. (these, by, photos, taken, are, Andy)

→ _____

4 그녀는 주방에서 요리하고 있는 남자를 가리켰다. (pointed to, in the kitchen, the man, she, cooking)

→ _____

5 그 사고에서 부상당한 사람들은 병원에 있다. (injured, in the hospital, the people, in the accident, are)

→ _____

6 브이 자를 하고 있는 남자아이는 Brian이다. (Brian, the boy, is, making, a V sign)

→ _____

B 빈칸 완성   우리말과 일치하도록 괄호 안의 말을 이용하여 빈칸에 알맞은 말을 쓰시오.

1 나는 고장 난 컴퓨터를 그에게 가져갔다. (break, computer)

→ I brought the _____ _____ to him.

2 우리는 어젯밤에 캠핑을 하는 동안 유성을 봤다. (shoot, star)

→ We saw a _____ _____ while camping last night.

3 무대에서 공연하고 있는 남자는 Dave이다. (perform, man)

→ The _____ _____ on stage is Dave.

4 우리는 올해 지어진 집으로 이사했다. (build, house)

→ We moved into a _____ _____ this year.

5 일요일 아침에 출발하는 비행기가 있나요? (depart, flight)

→ Is there a _____ _____ on Sunday morning?

6 이것은 나팔꽃이라고 불리는 꽃이다. (call, flower)

→ This is a _____ _____ morning glory.

C 문장 완성 · 우리말과 일치하도록 괄호 안의 말을 이용하여 문장을 완성하시오.

1 나는 점심으로 생선 튀김을 주문했다 (order, fish, fry)

→ _____ for lunch.

2 그는 떨어지는 빗소리를 좋아한다. (the sound of, rain, fall)

→ He likes _____ .

3 저쪽에서 노래를 하고 있는 남자를 봐. (the man, sing, over there)

→ Look at _____ .

4 나는 〈Love and War〉라는 제목의 책을 읽었다. (the book, title)

→ I read _____ .

5 우회전하고 있는 저 차를 따라가세요. (that car, turn right)

→ Follow _____ .

6 이것은 나의 할머니가 만드신 쿠키이다. (cookies, make, by, grandmother)

→ These are _____ .

D 오류 수정 · 밑줄 친 부분을 바르게 고쳐 문장을 다시 쓰시오.

1 The man <u>asked</u> me a question was a police officer. (나에게 질문을 한 남자는 경찰관이었다.)

→ _____

2 The car <u>parking</u> outside is my uncle's. (밖에 주차되어 있는 차는 나의 삼촌의 것이다.)

→ _____

3 The hero escaped in a <u>fly</u> car. (그 영웅은 하늘을 나는 자동차를 타고 탈출했다.)

→ _____

4 I received a letter <u>wrote</u> in English. (나는 영어로 쓰인 편지 한 통을 받았다.)

→ _____

5 The boy <u>kicks</u> the ball is my friend. (공을 차고 있는 소년은 내 친구이다.)

→ _____

6 The flowers <u>planting</u> in the spring are blooming now. (봄에 심은 꽃들이 지금 피어 나고 있다.)

→ _____

주의해야 할 분사

GRAMMAR FOCUS

① 감정을 나타내는 분사

감정과 관련된 타동사는 분사형으로 자주 쓰인다. '~한 감정을 일으키는'의 의미일 때는 현재분사를, '~한 감정을 느끼는'의 의미일 때는 과거분사를 사용한다.

The topic *interests* students. 그 주제는 학생들의 **흥미를 끈다.**

→ The topic is **interesting**. 그 주제는 **흥미롭다.**

→ Students are **interested** in the topic. 학생들은 그 주제에 **흥미를 느낀다.**

The news *surprised* everyone. 그 소식은 모두를 **놀라게 했다.**

→ The news was **surprising**. 그 소식은 **놀라웠다.**

→ Everyone was **surprised**. 모두가 **놀랐다.**

The test results *disappointed* Kate. 그 시험 결과는 Kate를 **실망시켰다.**

→ The test results were **disappointing**. 그 시험 결과는 **실망스러웠다.**

→ Kate was **disappointed**. Kate는 **실망했다.**

② 감정을 나타내는 동사의 분사형

- exciting (흥미진진한) – excited (흥분한, 신이 난)
- interesting (흥미로운) – interested (흥미를 느끼는)
- boring (지루한) – bored (지루해하는)
- tiring (피곤하게 하는) – tired (피곤한)
- relaxing (편안하게 하는) – relaxed (편안한)
- annoying (짜증나게 하는) – annoyed (짜증난)
- surprising (놀라운) – surprised (놀란)
- shocking (충격적인) – shocked (충격을 받은)
- satisfying (만족스러운) – satisfied (만족한)
- disappointing (실망스러운) – disappointed (실망한)
- embarrassing (당황스러운) – embarrassed (당황한)
- depressing (우울하게 하는) – depressed (우울한)

EXERCISE **A** 괄호 안에서 알맞은 것을 고르시오.

1 The people at the festival look (excited, exciting).

2 I read an (interested, interesting) article yesterday.

3 The constant noise was very (annoyed, annoying).

4 Jonathan is (satisfied, satisfying) with his job.

5 The concert last night was (disappointed, disappointing).

6 His lecture was (bored, boring) to most students.

7 Taking a walk in nature is (relaxed, relaxing).

8 Running your own business is (tired, tiring) but worthwhile.

9 Most people were (shocked, shocking) when they heard the news.

10 Some people feel (embarrassed, embarrassing) about being in public.

EXERCISE
B

우리말과 일치하도록 괄호 안의 말을 이용하여 문장을 완성하시오.

1 그의 연기는 매우 실망스러웠다. (disappoint)

→ His performance was very _____.

2 나는 그 이야기의 결말에 충격을 받았다. (shock)

→ I was _____ by the ending of the story.

3 그들은 경기에서 졌을 때 우울함을 느꼈다. (depress)

→ They felt _____ when they lost the game.

4 가족 휴가는 언제나 편안함을 준다. (relax)

→ A family vacation is always _____.

5 그녀의 이름을 잊어버린 것은 당황스러웠다. (embarrass)

→ Forgetting her name was _____.

6 그녀는 그 아이들이 너무 시끄럽게 해서 짜증이 났다. (annoy)

→ She was _____ because the kids were making a lot of noise.

EXERCISE
C

우리말과 일치하도록 〈보기〉에서 알맞은 동사를 골라 분사 형태로 바꿔 문장을 완성하시오.

보기	surprise	satisfy	shock	interest	tire

1 그 호텔의 모든 서비스가 만족스러웠다.

→ Every service at the hotel was _____.

2 그 사고를 봤을 때 나는 놀랐다.

→ I was _____ when I saw the accident.

3 그는 현대 건축에 관심이 있다.

→ He is _____ in modern architecture.

4 나는 시험이 끝난 후에 피곤함을 느꼈다.

→ I felt _____ after the exam was over.

5 지진에 대한 그 소식은 충격적이었다.

→ The news about the earthquake was _____.

WRITING FOCUS

A 배열 영작   우리말과 일치하도록 괄호 안의 말을 바르게 배열하시오.

1 그 축구 경기는 흥미진진했다. (the, exciting, soccer game, was)

→ _____

2 나는 내 성적에 실망했다. (disappointed, I, my, grades, was, with)

→ _____

3 그 뮤지컬은 조금 지루했다. (the, a little, musical, was, boring)

→ _____

4 학생들은 새 구내식당에 만족했다. (satisfied, were, with, students, the new cafeteria)

→ _____

5 Julia는 자신의 상황에 대해 우울해했다. (depressed, Julia, her, situation, was, about)

→ _____

6 산에서 바라보는 경치는 놀라웠다. (the, view, was, from, the, amazing, mountain)

→ _____

B 빈칸 완성   우리말과 일치하도록 빈칸에 알맞은 말을 쓰시오.

1 그들은 그 과학 실험에 흥미를 느꼈다. (interest)

→ They were _____ in the science experiment.

2 요가를 하는 것은 나를 편안하게 만든다. (relax)

→ Doing yoga makes me _____.

3 너에게 말해 줄 놀라운 소식이 있어. (surprise, news)

→ I have some _____ _____ to tell you.

4 그 중식당의 음식은 만족스러웠다. (satisfy)

→ The food at the Chinese restaurant was _____.

5 Tony는 피곤한 하루를 보냈다. (tire, day)

→ Tony had a _____ _____.

6 그는 당황스러운 상황에 처한 자신을 발견했다. (embarrass, situation)

→ He found himself in an _____ _____.

C 문장 완성   우리말과 일치하도록 괄호 안의 말을 이용하여 문장을 완성하시오.

1 Sandra는 그의 반응에 당황했다. (embarrass)

→ _____ by his reaction.

2 나는 캠핑 여행을 다녀온 후 피곤함을 느꼈다. (feel, tire)

→ _____ after the camping trip.

3 그 지루해하는 학생은 수업 중에 잠이 들었다. (bore, student, fall asleep)

→ _____ during the class.

4 장마철은 우울함을 느끼게 할 수 있다. (can, depress)

→ The rainy season _____ .

5 그 결과는 그들에게 놀라운 것이었다. (the results, surprise)

→ _____ to them.

6 당신은 이 제품에 관심이 있습니까? (interest)

→ _____ in this product?

D 오류 수정   밑줄 친 부분을 바르게 고쳐 문장을 다시 쓰시오.

1 It is <u>excited</u> to travel to new places.

→ _____

2 We are <u>satisfying</u> with Mr. Kim's class.

→ _____

3 Climbing a mountain is <u>tired</u>.

→ _____

4 The job wasn't <u>interested</u>, so he decided to quit.

→ _____

5 I felt <u>scare</u> during the thunderstorm last night.

→ _____

6 She never looks <u>worrying</u> and is always confident.

→ _____

[01-03] 빈칸에 들어갈 말로 알맞은 것을 고르시오.

01

The _____ dog scared me.

① bark   ② barked
③ barking   ④ to bark
⑤ to barking

02

He is reading an email _____ in English.

① write   ② wrote
③ writing   ④ written
⑤ to write

03

The event was _____, so we left early.

① disappoint   ② disappointed
③ disappointing   ④ to disappoint
⑤ to disappointing

04 밑줄 친 부분의 쓰임이 나머지 넷과 다른 것은?

① Don't wake up the sleeping baby.
② The car is making a strange sound.
③ Her hobby is watching classic movies.
④ We saw some people painting the wall.
⑤ Do you know the girl sitting next to Tom?

05 우리말과 일치하도록 주어진 말을 배열할 때, 세 번째로 오는 단어는?

차에서 기다리고 있는 남자는 나의 삼촌이다.
(the, uncle, man, in, car, my, is, the, waiting)

① in   ② car   ③ the
④ man   ⑤ waiting

[06-07] 밑줄 친 부분이 어법상 틀린 것을 고르시오.

06 ① Fried chicken is my favorite food.
② My cellphone has a broken screen.
③ Put the noodles in the boiling water.
④ Look at the boy wearing the blue cap.
⑤ The man come toward us is Mr. White.

07 ① The book has many touching stories.
② Tim was tired after he studied all day.
③ The movie made me very depressing.
④ The customer service wasn't satisfying.
⑤ The annoyed passenger got off the bus.

고난도
08 어법상 올바른 문장의 개수는?

ⓐ Daniel had a relaxed vacation.
ⓑ He lives in a house build in the forest.
ⓒ The kids are playing on the fallen leaves.
ⓓ The people sat at the table are my family.
ⓔ The street performance was interesting to watch.

① 1개   ② 2개   ③ 3개
④ 4개   ⑤ 5개

✏️ 서술형

09 빈칸에 들어갈 말을 〈보기〉에서 골라 알맞은 형태로 쓰시오. (단, 한 번씩만 쓸 것)

보기	make	serve	walk

(1) The man _____ the dog is my neighbor.

(2) The little girl gave me a ring _____ of clay.

(3) The dishes _____ at the restaurant were delicious.

10 우리말과 일치하도록 주어진 말을 바르게 배열하시오.

(1) 경찰이 발견한 그 차는 Cooper 씨의 것이다.
(the, found, the, by, car, police)

→ _____

is Mr. Cooper's.

(2) 누군가 싱크대에 수도꼭지를 틀어 놓았다.
(tap, left, somebody, the, running)

→ _____

in the sink.

11 두 문장을 분사를 이용하여 한 문장으로 연결하시오

(1) I know the woman. She is dancing to the music.

→ I know the woman _____ _____

_____ _____.

(2) He handed me a gift. It was wrapped in paper.

→ He handed me a gift _____

_____ _____.

12 어법상 틀린 부분을 찾아 바르게 고치시오.

(1) The cloth covered the table is colorful.

_____ → _____

(2) I received unexpecting package this morning.

_____ → _____

13 주어진 말을 활용하여 문장을 완성하시오.

(1) The long hike was _____, but I enjoyed it. (tire)

(2) The _____ children opened their Christmas presents. (excite)

14 우리말과 일치하도록 〈보기〉에서 필요한 단어들만 골라 배열하여 문장을 완성하시오. (중복 사용 가능)

보기	we	were	the	heard	news
		shocking		shocked	

(1) 우리는 TV에서 충격적인 뉴스를 들었다.

→ _____

on TV.

(2) 우리는 그 뉴스를 듣고 충격을 받았다.

→ _____

to hear the news.

15 그림을 보고, 주어진 말과 분사를 사용하여 문장을 완성하시오.

(1)

(2)

(1) The girl _____ on the stage is my sister. (sing)

(2) Look at the house _____ by the earthquake. (damage)

16 우리말과 일치하도록 〈보기〉에서 필요한 단어들만 골라 배열하여 문장을 완성하시오.

버스를 기다리는 그 남자는 지루해 보인다.

보기 the man   looks   waiting   waited
for a bus   boring   bored

→ _____

17 우리말과 일치하도록 주어진 말을 활용하여 문장을 완성하시오.

A: I just watched the new mystery movie.
B: Oh, did you like it?
A: Yes, it was great! 끝에 놀라운 반전이 있었거든. (surprise, twist)

→ There was a _____ at the end.

18 어법상 틀린 문장 2개를 골라 기호를 쓰고, 틀린 부분을 바르게 고치시오.

ⓐ The loud noise outside is annoyed.
ⓑ Kate doesn't look satisfied with her job.
ⓒ He asked me an embarrassing question.
ⓓ Look at the children made a snowman.
ⓔ The movies directed by him won many awards.

(   ) _____ → _____
(   ) _____ → _____

[19-20] 다음 글을 읽고, 물음에 답하시오.

A: How did you spend your vacation?
B: It was fun. I learned scuba diving.
A: Wow, that sounds excited! How was it?
B: I was a bit scared at first, but 그것은 흥미로운 경험이었어.

고난도

19 대화를 읽고, 어법상 틀린 부분을 찾아 바르게 고치시오.

_____ → _____

20 밑줄 친 우리말과 일치하도록 〈조건〉에 맞게 문장을 완성하시오.

조건 1. it, interest, experience를 활용할 것
2. 총 5단어로 쓸 것

→ _____

Chapter 07

수동태

1 능동태 vs. 수동태

능동태는 '~가 …하다'의 의미로 주어가 동작의 주체일 때 사용하고, 수동태는 '~가 …되다'의 의미로 주어가 동작의 대상일 때 사용한다. 수동태는 동사를 「be동사 + p.p.」 형태로 쓰고, 행위자는 동사 뒤에 「by + 목적격」으로 나타낸다.

| 능동태 | The workers | **build** | the house. | 일꾼들이 그 집을 **짓는다.** |
| 수동태 | The house | **is built** | **by** the workers. | 그 집은 일꾼들에 **의해 지어진다.** |

2 수동태 만드는 법

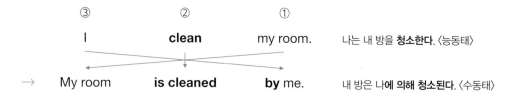

③ 능동태의 목적어를 주어 자리에 놓는다. (목적격 대명사는 주격으로 바꿈)
② 동사는 「be동사 + p.p.」 형태로 바꾼다. (be동사는 인칭, 수, 시제에 맞게 사용)
③ 능동태의 주어를 「by + 목적격」으로 쓴다.

3 수동태의 시제

수동태의 현재, 과거, 미래시제를 나타낼 때는 수동태의 be동사를 알맞은 시제로 바꾼다.

(1) 현재시제: am/is/are + p.p.

| | John Hunt | **coaches** | the team. | John Hunt가 그 팀을 지도한다. |
| → | The team | **is coached** | **by** John Hunt. | 그 팀은 John Hunt에 의해 지도된다. |

(2) 과거시제: was/were + p.p.

| | My sister | **wrote** | the poem. | 내 여동생이 그 시를 썼다. |
| → | The poem | was **written** | **by** my sister. | 그 시는 내 여동생에 의해 쓰였다. |

(3) 미래시제: will be + p.p.

| | Sue | **will bake** | the cake. | Sue가 그 케이크를 구울 것이다. |
| → | The cake | will be **made** | **by** Sue. | 그 케이크는 Sue에 의해 구워질 것이다. |

EXERCISE A

괄호 안에서 알맞은 것을 고르시오.

1 He (makes, is made) the best pasta in town.

2 The light bulb (invented, was invented) by Thomas Edison.

3 This room (will use, will be used) by guests.

4 The TV program (is watching, is watched) by many people.

5 Dinner was prepared by (they, them).

EXERCISE B

다음 문장을 수동태로 바꿔 쓰시오.

1 A lot of tourists visit the city.

→ The city _____ _____ _____ a lot of tourists.

2 She designed the beautiful dress.

→ The beautiful dress _____ _____ _____ her.

3 The students will open the box.

→ The box _____ _____ _____ _____ the students.

4 My parents grow these vegetables.

→ These vegetables _____ _____ _____ my parents.

EXERCISE C

우리말과 일치하도록 괄호 안의 말을 이용하여 문장을 완성하시오.

1 영어는 Taylor 선생님이 가르치신다. (teach)

→ English _____ _____ _____ Mr. Taylor.

2 이 그림은 1900년대에 유명한 화가에 의해 그려졌다. (paint)

→ This picture _____ _____ _____ a famous artist in the 1900s.

3 그 차는 여행하는 동안 Ann이 운전할 것이다. (drive)

→ The car _____ _____ _____ _____ Ann during the trip.

4 이 수납장들은 우리 할아버지께서 만드신 것이다. (make)

→ These cabinets _____ _____ _____ my grandfather.

WRITING FOCUS

A 배열 영작   우리말과 일치하도록 괄호 안의 말을 바르게 배열하시오.

1 그 긴급 통화 서비스는 시민들에 의해 사용된다. (used, the, is, citizens, emergency phone service, by)

→ _____

2 도서관 책들은 사서들에 의해 정리된다. (library books, librarians, by, organized, are)

→ _____

3 그 책은 John Smith에 의해 쓰였다. (the, by, book, written, John Smith, was)

→ _____

4 그 접시들은 우리가 닦았다. (the, were, by, dishes, washed, us)

→ _____

5 그 노래는 Emily에 의해 불릴 것이다. (Emily, the, sung, song, be, will, by)

→ _____

6 모든 식사는 그 주방장에 의해 준비될 것이다. (all, chef, will, the, prepared, meals, be, by)

→ _____

B 문장 전환   다음 문장을 수동태 문장으로 바꿔 쓰시오.

1 My brother and I clean our room.

→ _____

2 The florist decorates the tables.

→ _____

3 A car hit the tree last night.

→ _____

4 The Romans built the buildings.

→ _____

5 They will solve the problem.

→ _____

6 The manager will change the schedule.

→ _____

C 문장 완성 　우리말과 일치하도록 괄호 안의 말을 이용하여 수동태 문장을 완성하시오.

1 시장은 시민들에 의해 선출된다. (elect, citizens)

→ The mayor _____ .

2 그 시험은 Brown 선생님에 의해 채점된다. (grade, Mr. Brown)

→ The exams _____ .

3 그 컴퓨터는 John에 의해 고쳐졌다. (fix)

→ The computer _____ .

4 이 사진들은 Alan에 의해 찍혔다. (take)

→ These photos _____ .

5 그 무거운 상자는 로봇에 의해 옮겨질 것이다. (move, a robot)

→ The heavy box _____ .

6 그 나무들은 자원봉사자들에 의해 심어질 것이다. (plant, volunteers)

→ The trees _____ .

D 오류 수정 　밑줄 친 부분을 바르게 고쳐 문장을 다시 쓰시오.

1 They <u>help</u> by the government. (그들은 정부의 도움을 받는다.)

→ _____

2 The tornado <u>was destroyed</u> trees and houses. (그 토네이도는 나무와 집들을 파괴했다.)

→ _____

3 This app <u>used</u> by many people. (이 앱은 많은 사람들에 의해 사용된다.)

→ _____

4 Music <u>will be play</u> by the band. (음악은 그 밴드에 의해 연주될 것이다.)

→ _____

5 *Hamlet* <u>was wrote</u> by Shakespeare. (〈햄릿〉은 셰익스피어에 의해 쓰였다.)

→ _____

6 The car was designed <u>by he</u>. (그 자동차는 그에 의해 설계되었다.)

→ _____

① **수동태의 부정문**

수동태의 부정문은 「be동사 + not + p.p.」 형태로 쓴다.

Mr. Green	**doesn't teach**	us.	Green 선생님은 우리를 **가르치지 않으신다**.
→ We	**aren't taught**	by Mr. Green.	우리는 Green 선생님에게 **배우지 않는다**.

He **didn't directed** this movie. 그는 이 영화를 감독하지 않았다.

→ This movie **wasn't directed** by him. 이 영화는 그에 의해 감독되지 않았다.

② **수동태의 의문문**

수동태의 의문문은 「Be동사 + 주어 + p.p. ~?」 형태로 쓴다.

Do	they	**wash**	the car?	그들은 그 차를 **세차하니**?
→ Is	the car	**washed**	by them?	그 차는 그들에 의해 **세차되니**?

Did she **break** the record? 그녀는 그 기록을 깼니?

→ **Was** the record **broken** by her? 그 기록은 그녀에 의해 깨졌니?

③ **조동사가 있는 문장의 수동태**

조동사가 있는 문장의 수동태는 「조동사 + be + p.p.」 형태로 쓴다.

Anyone	**can use**	the library.	누구나 그 도서관을 **이용할 수 있다**.
→ The library	**can be used**	by anyone.	그 도서관은 누구에게나 **이용될 수 있다**.

John **may buy** the car. John은 그 차를 구입할지도 모른다.

→ The car **may be bought** by John. 그 차는 John에 의해 구입될지도 모른다.

cf. 조동사가 있는 문장의 수동태 부정문은 「조동사 + not + be + p.p.」로 나타낸다.

Children **should not drink** energy drinks. 아이들은 에너지 드링크를 마시면 안 된다.

→ Energy drinks **should not be drunk** by children. 에너지 드링크는 아이들이 마시면 안 된다.

A 괄호 안에서 알맞은 것을 고르시오.

1 The room (is not, does not) cleaned by Louise.

2 The cookies (were not, did not) eaten by me.

3 (Did, Was) the thief caught by the police?

4 Where were the keys (find, found) by Sarah?

5 The car (can fixed, can be fixed) by the mechanic.

6 This medicine (must be not, must not be) taken by children.

EXERCISE B

다음 문장을 수동태로 바꿔 쓰시오.

1 I do not wear these jeans anymore.

→ These jeans _____ _____ _____ by me anymore.

2 Thomas Edison did not invent the telephone.

→ The telephone _____ _____ _____ by Thomas Edison.

3 Do many people visit the museum?

→ _____ the museum _____ by many people?

4 Did Judy send the email?

→ _____ the email _____ by Judy?

5 He can solve the math problem.

→ The math problem _____ _____ _____ by him.

6 Anyone should not waste water.

→ Water _____ _____ _____ _____ by anyone.

EXERCISE C

우리말과 일치하도록 괄호 안의 말을 이용하여 문장을 완성하시오.

1 이 컴퓨터는 내가 사용하지 않는다. (use)

→ This computer _____ _____ _____ by me.

2 그 파일은 그녀가 다운로드하지 않았다. (download)

→ This file _____ _____ _____ by her.

3 이 책들은 학생들이 자주 읽나요? (read)

→ _____ these books often _____ by students?

4 이 보고서는 Tom에 의해 쓰여졌니? (write)

→ _____ this report _____ by Tom?

5 새로운 건물이 그들에 의해 지어질지도 모른다. (may, build)

→ A new building _____ _____ _____ by them.

6 그 축제는 금요일에 열리지 않을 것이다. (will, hold)

→ The festival _____ _____ _____ _____ on Friday.

WRITING FOCUS

A 배열 영작   우리말과 일치하도록 괄호 안의 말을 바르게 배열하시오. (수동태 문장으로 쓸 것)

1 공중전화는 많은 사람들에게 사용되지 않는다. (people, payphones, not, by, used, many, are)

→ _____

2 그의 질문은 누구에게도 답변되지 않았다. (answered, his, anyone, by, was, not, question)

→ _____

3 그 공은 Steve가 던졌니? (Steve, the, thrown, ball, was, by)

→ _____

4 그 작업은 인공지능에 의해 수행되나요? (the, is, AI, performed, by, task)

→ _____

5 그 규칙들은 학생들에 의해 지켜져야 한다. (rules, the, be, students, followed, must, by)

→ _____

6 그 행사는 주최측에 의해 연기될 지도 모른다. (the, may, event, postponed, the, by, be, host)

→ _____

B 빈칸 완성   우리말과 일치하도록 괄호 안의 말을 이용하여 빈칸에 알맞은 말을 쓰시오.

1 나는 Tom의 파티에 초대받지 못했다. (invite)

→ I _____ _____ _____ to the party by Tom.

2 그 농작물은 폭풍으로 인한 피해를 입지 않았다. (damage)

→ The crops _____ _____ _____ by the storm.

3 그 개는 Andrew가 목욕시키니? (wash)

→ _____ the dog _____ by Andrew?

4 정원의 꽃들은 그녀가 심었니? (plant)

→ _____ the flowers in the garden _____ by her?

5 우승자의 이름은 그에 의해 발표될 것이다. (announce)

→ The winner's name _____ _____ _____ by him.

6 그 환경 문제는 단일 국가에 의해 해결될 수 없다. (cannot, solve)

→ The environmental problem _____ _____ _____ by a single country.

C 문장 전환   다음 문장을 수동태 문장으로 바꿔 쓰시오.

1 They do not wash the dishes.

→ _____

2 I did not lock the door.

→ _____

3 Does a native speaker teach the English class?

→ _____

4 Did Ann write the card?

→ _____

5 John should do the homework.

→ _____

6 He must pay the bill today.

→ _____

D 오류 수정   어법상 틀린 부분을 바르게 고쳐 문장을 다시 쓰시오.

1 This package was not send by Paul. (이 소포는 Paul이 보낸 것이 아니다.)

→ _____

2 The books did not bought by me. (그 책들은 내가 사지 않았다.)

→ _____

3 Did this picture painted by Sue? (이 그림은 Sue가 그렸니?)

→ _____

4 Are many people visited the website? (많은 사람들이 그 웹사이트를 방문합니까?)

→ _____

5 The movie can be watching by all ages. (그 영화는 전 연령대가 볼 수 있다.)

→ _____

6 The construction may not completed until June. (그 공사는 6월까지 완료되지 않을지도 모른다.)

→ _____

① **by 이외의 전치사를 사용하는 경우**

수동태에서 행위자를 나타낼 때 주로 by를 쓰지만, 일부 동사들을 다른 전치사를 사용한다.

· be filled with	~로 가득 차다	· be interested in	~에 관심[흥미]이 있다
· be covered with	~로 덮이다	· be tired of	~에 싫증나다[지치다]
· be satisfied with	~에 만족하다	· be known to	~에게 알려져 있다
· be pleased with	~에 기뻐하다[만족하다]	· be known for	~로 알려져 있다[유명하다]
· be excited about	~에 흥분하다[들뜨다]	· be made of	~로 만들어지다 (물리적 변화)
· be worried about	~에 대해 걱정하다	· be made from	~로 만들어지다 (화학적 변화)

The playground **is covered with** snow. 그 운동장은 눈으로 덮여 있다.

I **am satisfied with** my job. 나는 내 직업에 만족한다.

Picasso's works **are known to** many people. 피카소의 작품은 많은 사람들에게 알려져 있다.

The restaurant **is known for** its French cuisine. 그 식당은 프랑스 요리로 유명하다.

The table **is made of** wood. 그 식탁은 나무로 만들어졌다.

Cheese **is made from** milk. 치즈는 우유로 만들어진다.

② **「by + 행위자」의 생략**

(1) 행위자가 일반인일 때

English and Chinese **are spoken** in Hong Kong. 영어와 중국어는 홍콩에서 쓰인다.

This song **is loved** all over the world. 이 노래는 전 세계에서 사랑받는다.

(2) 행위자를 알 수 없거나 중요하지 않을 때

My bag **was stolen** on the bus. 내 가방은 버스에서 도난당했다.

The watch **is made** in Switzerland. 그 시계는 스위스에서 만들어졌다.

EXERCISE
A

괄호 안에서 알맞은 것을 고르시오.

1 The bookshelf is covered (by, with) dust.

2 My parents were so pleased (at, with) my grades.

3 He is excited (about, of) the new job opportunity.

4 Are you satisfied (for, with) the food?

5 Sarah is interested (at, in) fashion.

6 Gary is worried (about, in) making new friends.

7 Marshmallows are made (from, of) sugar.

8 Busan is known (for, to) its amazing night views.

EXERCISE B

〈보기〉에서 알맞은 전치사를 골라 문장을 완성하시오. (중복 사용 가능)

보기	with	in	of	for	to	from

1 The chairs are made _____ wood and fabric.

2 I was not pleased _____ his rude behavior.

3 She is very interested _____ classical music.

4 The basket was filled _____ fresh apples.

5 I am tired _____ hearing the same old stories.

6 Rome is known _____ its historical landmarks.

7 The truth will be known _____ everybody soon.

8 Most customers are satisfied _____ our service.

9 Butter and yogurt are made _____ milk.

10 The floor is covered _____ a thick carpet.

EXERCISE C

우리말과 일치하도록 괄호 안의 말을 이용하여 문장을 완성하시오.

1 Kevin은 집에 홀로 남겨졌다. (leave)

→ Kevin _____ _____ home alone.

2 크리스마스 캐럴은 많은 나라에서 불린다. (sing)

→ Christmas carols _____ _____ in many countries.

3 프랑스어는 캐나다 일부 지역에서 쓰인다. (speak)

→ French _____ _____ in some parts of Canada.

4 올림픽 경기는 4년마다 개최된다. (hold)

→ The Olympic Games _____ _____ every four years.

5 그 사원은 400년 전에 지어졌다. (build)

→ The temple _____ _____ 400 years ago.

6 그녀의 책들은 도서관에서 도난당했다. (steal)

→ Her books _____ _____ in the library.

WRITING FOCUS

A 배열 영작   우리말과 일치하도록 괄호 안의 말을 바르게 배열하시오.

1 그는 요리에 관심이 없다. (interested, he, in, not, cooking, is)

→ _____

2 Mary는 그녀의 첫 해외여행에 들떠 있다. (Mary, excited, abroad, is, about, her first trip)

→ _____

3 우리는 그 식당에서의 식사에 만족했다. (the, we, with, meal, were, at the restaurant, satisfied)

→ _____

4 그의 선행은 모두에게 알려져 있다. (everyone, his, known, good behavior, to, is)

→ _____

5 내 자전거는 공원에서 도난당했다. (my, was, bike, in the park, stolen)

→ _____

6 우승자는 온라인 투표를 통해 선정될 것이다. (will, the, winner, chosen, be, through online voting)

→ _____

B 빈칸 완성   우리말과 일치하도록 빈칸에 알맞은 말을 쓰시오.

1 나는 그의 건강이 걱정된다. (worry)

→ I _____ _____ _____ his health.

2 이 핸드백은 가죽으로 만들어졌다. (make)

→ This handbag _____ _____ _____ leather.

3 그 식당은 해산물 요리로 유명하다. (know)

→ The restaurant _____ _____ _____ its seafood dishes

4 그 산들은 일년 내내 눈으로 덮여 있다. (cover)

→ The mountains _____ _____ _____ snow all year round.

5 쓰레기는 일주일에 두 번 수거된다. (collect)

→ The garbage _____ _____ twice a week.

6 모든 티켓이 단 한 시간 만에 판매되었다. (sell)

→ All the tickets _____ _____ in just an hour.

C 문장 완성 우리말과 일치하도록 괄호 안의 말을 이용하여 문장을 완성하시오.

1 초콜릿은 코코아 열매로 만들어진다. (make, cocoa beans)

→ Chocolate _____ .

2 그 욕조는 따뜻한 물로 가득 차 있다. (fill, warm water)

→ The bathtub _____ .

3 그는 장거리 출장에 싫증이 났다. (tire, long business trips)

→ He _____ .

4 이 와인은 프랑스에서 생산되었다. (produce, in France)

→ This wine _____ .

5 그 다리는 1980년에 지어졌다. (build, in 1980)

→ The bridge _____ .

6 새로운 회장이 내년에 선출될 것이다. (will, elect, next year)

→ A new president _____ .

D 오류 수정 어법상 틀린 부분을 바르게 고쳐 문장을 다시 쓰시오.

1 Do you interested in Korean culture? (너는 한국 문화에 관심이 있니?)

→ _____

2 They were not satisfied on the final score. (그들은 최종 점수에 만족하지 못했다.)

→ _____

3 His novel is known for many people. (그의 소설은 많은 사람들에게 알려져 있다.)

→ _____

4 You don't have to be worried for it. (너는 그것에 대해 걱정할 필요가 없어.)

→ _____

5 The wallet was found to a passerby. (그 지갑은 한 행인에 의해 발견되었다.)

→ _____

6 The letter was sent by the wrong address. (그 편지는 잘못된 주소로 발송되었다.)

→ _____

ACTUAL TEST

01 빈칸에 들어갈 말로 알맞은 것은?

Bill _____ by a mosquito.

① bite
② bitten
③ is biting
④ has bitten
⑤ was bitten

02 대화의 빈칸에 들어갈 말로 알맞은 것은?

A: Who _____ this photo?
B: It _____ my sister.

① takes – took
② took – was took
③ took – was taken by
④ was taken by – took
⑤ was taken – was taken by

03 우리말을 영어로 바르게 옮긴 것은?

이 그림은 Jane에 의해 그려지지 않았다.

① Jane did not painted by this picture.
② Jane was not painted by this picture.
③ This picture did not painted by Jane.
④ This picture was not painted by Jane.
⑤ This picture were not painted by Jane.

04 우리말과 일치하도록 주어진 말을 배열할 때, 네 번째로 오는 단어는?

그녀의 반지는 침대 밑에서 발견되었다.
(found, her, was, under, ring, bed, the)

① the
② was
③ ring
④ under
⑤ found

05 빈칸에 들어갈 수 있는 말이 <u>아닌</u> 것은?

• She is satisfied _____ her new job.
• I am tired _____ waiting for the bus.
• He is interested _____ ancient history.
• She is always worried _____ her health.

① in
② at
③ of
④ with
⑤ about

06 주어진 문장을 수동태로 바르게 바꾼 것은?

① The ball hit Peter.
　→ Peter was hitted by the ball.
② The boy broke the window.
　→ The window is broken by the boy.
③ King Sejong invented Hangeul.
　→ Hangeul invented by King Sejong.
④ Amy bought this shirt yesterday.
　→ This shirt was bought yesterday.
⑤ People waste a lot of plastic each year.
　→ A lot of plastic is wasted each year.

07 밑줄 친 부분을 잘못 고친 것은?

ⓐ The game is played yesterday.
ⓑ This letter did not write by me.
ⓒ Did the room painted by Peter?
ⓓ The plants are watered my father.
ⓔ When will the computer is repaired?

① ⓐ - was played
② ⓑ - was not wrote
③ ⓒ - Was
④ ⓓ - by my father
⑤ ⓔ - be repaired

고난도

08 어법상 올바른 문장의 개수는?

ⓐ Cats are loving by many people.
ⓑ We were not invited to the party.
ⓒ Did your sister draw this cartoon?
ⓓ The homework was done to John.
ⓔ *Yesterday* was sang by the Beatles.
ⓕ The report must be finished by Friday.

① 1개   ② 2개   ③ 3개
④ 4개   ⑤ 5개

11 어법상 틀린 부분을 찾아 바르게 고치시오.

(1) Tom was given this book to me.

_____ → _____

(2) This sweater made by my grandmother.

_____ → _____

12 빈칸에 수동태를 사용하여 대화를 완성하시오.

A: Did you bake these cookies yourself?
B: No, I didn't. They _____
_____ _____ my mom.

✎ 서술형

09 주어진 말을 활용하여 문장을 완성하시오.

(1) Disneyland _____ by
many people every year. (visit)

(2) A surprise party _____
for me yesterday. (throw)

(3) The clothes _____ to the
charity next week. (will, send)

[13-15] 주어진 문장을 수동태로 바꿔 쓰시오.

13

Some students do not understand the lesson.

→ _____

14

Did James eat the cake?

→ _____

10 주어진 말을 바르게 배열하여 문장을 완성하시오.
(단, 필요시 형태를 바꿀 것)

(1) 〈로미오와 줄리엣〉은 셰익스피어에 의해 쓰였다.
(write, Shakespeare, by, be)

→ *Romeo and Juliet* _____

_____.

(2) 피라미드는 고대 이집트인들에 의해 지어졌다.
(build, be, ancient Egyptians, by)

→ The pyramids _____

_____.

15

Anyone must not open the door.

→ _____

16 그림을 보고, 〈조건〉에 맞게 문장을 완성하시오.

> **조건** 1. decorate, they, the Christmas tree를 활용할 것
> 2. (1)은 능동태, (2)는 수동태로 쓰되, 행위자를 반드시 포함할 것
> 3. 과거시제로 쓸 것

(1) _____

(2) _____

17 우리 가족의 가사 분담표를 보고, 〈예시〉와 같이 문장을 완성하시오.

Mom	do the laundry
Dad	clean the bathroom
I	clean the windows

> **예시** The laundry is done by Mom.

(1) _____

(2) _____

18 우리말과 일치하도록 주어진 말을 활용하여 문장을 완성하시오.

그들은 그 대회 결과에 만족하지 않았다. (satisfy)

→ _____ _____ _____

_____ _____ the results of the

competition.

[19-20] 다음 글을 읽고, 물음에 답하시오.

Sungnyemun Gate is Korea's National Treasure Number. 1. It ⓐwas built in 1398 as the entrance to the capital of the Joseon Dynasty. The gate ⓑis made of stone and wood and is the oldest wooden building in Seoul.

Unfortunately, a fire in 2008 destroyed this historic structure. After years of restoration work, it ⓒwas reopened to the public in 2013, and now people ⓓcan be enjoyed Sungnyemun Gate once again.

19 어법상 틀린 부분을 찾아 기호를 쓰고 바르게 고치시오.

(   ) → _____

20 밑줄 친 문장을 수동태로 바꿔 쓰시오.

→ Unfortunately, _____

_____ in 2008.

Chapter 08

대명사

GRAMMAR FOCUS

① one

부정대명사 one은 앞에서 언급한 명사와 같은 종류의 다른 하나를 가리킬 때 쓴다. 복수 명사는 ones로 대신한다.

I need *a stapler*. Do you have **one**? 나는 스테이플러가 필요해. 너에게 하나 있니?

His *glasses* are broken. He needs to buy new **ones**. 그의 안경은 깨졌다. 그는 새것을 사야 한다.

cf. 앞에서 언급한 바로 그 명사를 가리킬 때는 it을 쓴다.

I bought *a new coat*, and I like **it**. 나는 새 코트를 샀는데 그것이 마음에 든다.

② one, another, the other

one, another, the other는 정해진 범위 안에서 대상을 하나씩 언급할 때 쓴다.

one ~, the other... (둘 중) 하나는 ~, 나머지 하나는 ···	I have two balls. **One** is red, and **the other** is blue. 나는 공 두 개가 있다. **하나는** 빨간색이고 **나머지 하나는** 파란색이다.
one ~, another..., the other – (셋 중) 하나는 ~, 또 하나는 ···, 나머지 하나는 –	I have three balls. **One** is red, **another** is yellow, and **the other** is blue. 나는 공 세 개가 있다. **하나는** 빨간색, **또 하나는** 노란색, **나머지 하나는** 파란색이다.

cf. 둘 이상의 '나머지 모두'를 가리킬 때는 the others를 쓴다.

I have ten balls. **One** is red, and **the others** are blue. (하나는 ~, 나머지 모두는 ···)

I have ten balls. **One** is red, **another** is yellow, and **the others** are blue. (하나는 ~, 또 하나는 ···, 나머지 모두는 –)

③ some, others, the others

some, others, the others는 대상을 여러 개씩 묶어서 언급할 때 쓴다.

some ~, others... 일부는 ~, 다른 일부는 ···	**Some** are Korean, and **others** are Chinese. **일부는** 한국인이고, **다른 일부는** 중국인이다.
some ~, the others... 일부는 ~, 나머지 모두는 ···	**Some** are Korean, and **the others** are Chinese. **일부는** 한국인이고, **나머지 모두는** 중국인이다.

④ each, every, all, both

each, all, both는 대명사뿐 아니라 형용사로도 쓸 수 있는 반면, every는 형용사로만 쓸 수 있다.

each 각자, 각각(의)	단수 취급	**Each** *student* **has** a book. **Each of** *them* **has** a talent. *each of + 복수 명사 + 단수 동사	각 학생은 책을 가지고 있다. 그들 각자 재능이 있다.
every 모든	단수 취급	**Every** *student* **wears** a uniform. *every / each + 단수 명사 + 단수 동사	모든 학생은 교복을 입는다.
all 모두, 모든 (것)	주어에 따라 단수/복수 취급	**All (of)** the *food* **is** cold. **All (of)** the *apples* **are** fresh.	그 음식은 모두 식었다. 그 사과들은 모두 싱싱하다.
both 둘 다(의)	복수 취급	**Both** *books* **are** interesting. **Both of** *us* **are** tall.	두 책 모두 흥미롭다. 우리 둘 다 키가 크다.

EXERCISE **A** 괄호 안에서 알맞은 것을 고르시오.

1 Is this your new car? I love (it, one).

2 I lost my cellphone. I have to buy a new (it, one).

3 Your sneakers are worn out. I'll get some new (one, ones) for you.

4 I have two sisters. One lives in Seoul, and (other, the other) lives in Busan.

5 He has three pets. One is a dog, (one, another) is a cat, and the other is a goldfish.

6 (Some, Others) like action movies, and others like comedies.

7 (Each, All) flower has its own beauty.

8 Each of the balloons (have, has) a different color.

9 Every (boy is, boys are) wearing a name tag.

10 All the food at the party (was, were) delicious.

11 All the cookies in the basket (is, are) freshly baked.

12 Both (country, countries) want to trade with each other.

EXERCISE **B** 우리말과 일치하도록 〈보기〉에서 알맞은 말을 골라 문장을 완성하시오. (중복 사용 가능)

보기	each	all	both

1 모든 아이들이 궁금해하는 표정이다.

→ _____ the children look curious.

2 경주의 각 참가자는 메달을 받았다.

→ _____ participant in the race received a medal.

3 두 선택 모두 장점과 단점이 있다.

→ _____ options have advantages and disadvantages.

4 금고 안의 모든 돈은 그의 것이다.

→ _____ the money in the safe is his.

5 나의 부모님 두 분 다 매일 열심히 일하신다.

→ _____ of my parents work hard every day.

WRITING FOCUS

A 배열 영작 우리말과 일치하도록 괄호 안의 말을 바르게 배열하시오.

1 그들은 개가 있어. 나도 한 마리 키우고 싶어. (have, one, dog, a, have)

→ They _____. I want to _____, too.

2 한 명은 딸이고, 나머지 한 명은 아들이다. (one, a, other, daughter, is, a, the, is, son)

→ _____, and _____.

3 일부는 독일인이고, 나머지 모두는 프랑스인이다. (French, are, some, the, German, others, are)

→ _____, and _____.

4 내 친구들 모두가 내 생일 파티에 왔다. (all, my, of, came, friends)

→ _____ to my birthday party.

5 모든 시민은 투표할 권리가 있다. (citizen, the, every, has, right)

→ _____ to vote.

6 그 학생들 둘 다 수학을 잘 한다. (both, the, are, students, of, good)

→ _____ at math.

B 빈칸 완성 우리말과 일치하도록 빈칸에 알맞은 말을 쓰시오.

1 그녀는 새 원피스를 샀다. 나는 그것이 마음에 든다. (like)

→ She bought a new dress. I _____ _____.

2 한 권은 소설, 또 한 권은 만화책, 나머지 한 권은 전기이다. (be)

→ One is a novel, another is a comic book, and _____ _____ _____ a biography.

3 일부는 낚시하러 갔고, 다른 몇 명은 수영하러 갔다. (go)

→ _____ _____ fishing, and _____ _____ swimming.

4 저 방의 모든 가구는 나무로 만들어졌다. (be)

→ _____ the furniture in that room _____ made of wood.

5 각 축구팀은 11명의 선수들로 구성된다. (consist of)

→ _____ soccer team _____ _____ eleven players.

6 두 하키 선수 모두 캐나다인이다. (be)

→ _____ hockey players _____ Canadians.

C 문장 완성   우리말과 일치하도록 괄호 안의 말을 이용하여 문장을 완성하시오.

1 우리는 차가 필요해. 공항에서 한 대를 빌리자. (let's, rent)

→ We need a car. _____ at the airport.

2 한 명은 늦었지만, 나머지 모두는 제시간에 도착했다. (late, arrive)

→ _____, but _____ on time.

3 일부는 봄을 좋아하고, 다른 일부는 가을을 좋아한다. (like, spring, fall)

→ _____, and _____.

4 우리 각자 침실을 가지고 있다. (us, have)

→ _____ a bedroom.

5 그 여자아이들 모두 같은 학교에 다닌다. (the girls, go)

→ _____ to the same school.

6 그들 둘 다 서울에 산다. (them, live)

→ _____ in Seoul.

D 오류 수정   밑줄 친 부분을 바르게 고쳐 문장을 다시 쓰시오.

1 I need a pen. Can I borrow it? (나는 펜이 필요해. 내가 하나 빌릴 수 있을까?)

→ _____

2 One is a dog, other is a cat, and the other is a bird.

(하나는 개, 다른 하나는 고양이, 나머지 하나는 새이다.)

→ _____

3 Some are apples, and others are oranges. (일부는 사과이고, 나머지 모두는 오렌지이다.)

→ _____

4 Every students have a student ID card. (모든 학생은 학생증을 가지고 있다.)

→ _____

5 Each of the child has a special talent. (그 아이들 각자 특별한 재능이 있다.)

→ _____

6 Both team performed well in the game. (두 팀 모두 그 경기에서 잘했다.)

→ _____

GRAMMAR FOCUS

1 재귀대명사의 용법

재귀대명사는 인칭대명사의 소유격이나 목적격에 -self(단수)나 -selves(복수)를 붙인 형태로, myself, yourself, himself, herself, itself, ourselves, yourselves, themselves가 있다.

(1) 재귀 용법: '~ 자신'의 의미로, 주어와 목적어가 같을 때 목적어 자리에 쓴다. 이 경우 재귀대명사는 생략할 수 없다.

I love **myself**. 나는 **나 자신**을 사랑한다.

(2) 강조 용법: '직접, 스스로, ~ 자체'의 의미로, 주어나 목적어를 강조할 때 쓴다. 주로 강조하는 말 바로 뒤나 문장 끝에 쓰고, 이 경우 재귀대명사는 생략할 수 있다.

He **himself** solved the puzzle. 그가 **직접** 그 퍼즐을 풀었다.

The children cleaned their rooms **themselves**. 그 아이들은 **스스로** 그들의 방을 청소했다.

2 재귀대명사의 관용적 표현

· by oneself	혼자서	· enjoy oneself	즐거운 시간을 보내다
· for oneself	자신을 위해, 스스로	· hurt / cut / burn oneself	다치다 / 베이다 / 화상을 입다
· teach oneself	독학하다	· help oneself (to)	(~을) 마음껏 먹다
· talk to oneself	혼잣말을 하다	· behave oneself	예의 바르게 행동하다
· introduce oneself	자기소개를 하다	· make oneself at home	편하게 있다[지내다]

I completed the project **by myself**. 나는 **혼자서** 그 프로젝트를 완성했다.

She bought a dress **for herself**. 그녀는 **자신을 위해** 원피스 한 벌을 샀다.

He often **talks to himself** in the shower. 그는 종종 샤워할 때 **혼잣말을 한다**.

We **enjoyed ourselves** at the beach. 우리는 해변에서 **즐거운 시간을 보냈다**.

EXERCISE
A

괄호 안에서 알맞은 것을 고르시오.

1 You should believe in (you, yourself).

2 Thank (you, yourself) for your help, Julia.

3 I made breakfast for John and (me, myself).

4 I told (him, himself) about the accident.

5 Jack and I made a video clip for (us, ourselves).

6 They talk about (her, herself) all the time.

7 He needs to take better care of (him, himself).

8 They painted the room (them, themselves).

9 My dog is sick and can't feed (it, itself).

10 She was proud of (her, herself) after achieving her goal.

EXERCISE B

빈칸에 알맞은 재귀대명사를 쓰시오.

1 My grandfather lives by _____.

2 She set a goal for _____ this year.

3 Sometimes I talk to _____ in my room.

4 Please help _____ to some cake, Sam.

5 Be careful with the knife; you might hurt _____.

6 He and I introduced _____ to each other in class.

7 You guys, make _____ at home.

8 I burned _____ while I was cooking.

9 The children make their beds _____.

10 She decided to teach _____ how to code.

11 He always behaves _____ like a gentleman.

12 Mia and Paul enjoyed _____ during their summer vacation.

EXERCISE C

빈칸에 알맞은 재귀대명사를 써서 대화를 완성하시오.

1 A: I heard you had a car accident. Are you okay?

   B: I hurt _____ a little, but it is nothing serious.

2 A: Don't blame _____ for the mistake, Kevin.

   B: Thank you for your concern.

3 A: We made it to the finals _____.

   B: Congratulations!

4 A: How did she learn French?

   B: She taught _____ French.

5 A: George went to Europe by _____.

   B: He is very brave to go there alone.

6 A: Behave _____, or you will be in trouble.

   B: Okay, I will be more careful.

WRITING FOCUS

A 배열 영작 우리말과 일치하도록 괄호 안의 말을 바르게 배열하시오.

1 Helen은 그 실수에 대해 자책했다. (for, Helen, herself, the, blamed, mistake)

→ _____

2 나는 나 자신에게 화가 난다. (myself, am, with, I, angry)

→ _____

3 거울 속의 네 모습이 보이니? (see, you, in, yourself, the, can, mirror)

→ _____

4 Jones 씨는 혼자 일하는 것을 선호한다. (himself, to, prefers, by, Mr. Jones, work)

→ _____

5 우리는 우리의 성공을 자축했다. (congratulated, success, we, on, our, ourselves)

→ _____

6 아기들은 스스로 먹을 수 없다. (babies, feed, can't, themselves)

→ _____

B 빈칸 완성 우리말과 일치하도록 빈칸에 알맞은 재귀대명사를 쓰시오.

1 그는 오직 자신만 생각한다.

→ He only thinks about _____.

2 우리 엄마가 직접 이 화병을 만들었다.

→ My mom made this vase _____.

3 우리는 벽난로 곁에서 몸을 따뜻하게 했다.

→ We warmed _____ by the fireplace.

4 그 컴퓨터는 자동으로 고쳐졌다.

→ The computer fixed _____ automatically.

5 나는 내 사진 몇 장을 소셜 미디어에 올렸다.

→ I posted some pictures of _____ on social media.

6 모두 환영합니다. 들어오셔서 편히 계세요.

→ You are all welcome. Come on in and make _____ at home.

C 문장 완성   우리말과 일치하도록 괄호 안의 말과 재귀대명사를 이용하여 문장을 완성하시오.

1 나는 수건으로 몸을 닦았다. (dry, with a towel)

➡ _____

2 우리는 그 영화제에서 즐거운 시간을 보냈다. (enjoy, at the film festival)

➡ _____

3 그는 깨진 유리에 베었다. (cut, on the broken glass)

➡ _____

4 그녀는 수영하는 법을 스스로 배웠다. (teach, how to swim)

➡ _____

5 그들은 적들로부터 자신을 지켰다. (protect, from their enemies)

➡ _____

6 그는 심사 위원들에게 자기소개를 했다. (introduce, to the judges)

➡ _____

D 오류 수정   밑줄 친 부분을 바르게 고쳐 문장을 다시 쓰시오.

1 We should love ourself. (우리는 자신을 사랑해야 한다.)

➡ _____

2 The plan it is not bad. (그 계획 자체는 나쁘지 않다.)

➡ _____

3 Chris cut his hair itself. (Chris는 그의 머리카락을 직접 잘랐다.)

➡ _____

4 I'm looking for a shirt for me. (저는 제가 입을 셔츠를 찾고 있어요.)

➡ _____

5 The girls took a picture of herself. (그 여자아이들은 자신들의 사진을 찍었다.)

➡ _____

6 He often goes fishing of himself. (그는 종종 혼자서 낚시하러 간다.)

➡ _____

01 빈칸에 들어갈 말로 알맞은 것은?

I lost my earphones. I should buy some new _____.

① it
② one
③ ones
④ some
⑤ others

02 빈칸에 들어갈 말이 순서대로 짝지어진 것은?

- _____ flower is beautiful.
- _____ the cookies taste great.

① All – Each
② All – Both
③ Every – All
④ Both – Every
⑤ Each – Every

03 빈칸에 들어갈 수 없는 것을 모두 고르면?

Kate has three kittens. _____ is white, _____ is black, and _____ is orange.

① It[it]
② One[one]
③ Other[other]
④ Another[another]
⑤ The other[the other]

04 밑줄 친 부분과 바꿔 쓸 수 있는 것은?

We ordered three pizzas. One had pepperoni, and <u>two</u> had mushrooms.

① ones
② some
③ others
④ another
⑤ the others

05 밑줄 친 부분의 쓰임이 나머지 넷과 다른 것은?

① I am so proud of <u>myself</u>.
② She wrote a book about <u>herself</u>.
③ The magician hid <u>himself</u> in a box.
④ You should do your homework <u>yourself</u>.
⑤ Writing is a good way to express <u>ourselves</u>.

06 밑줄 친 부분의 의미가 바르지 않은 것은?

① He <u>talked to himself</u> quietly.
(혼잣말을 하다)
② I fell off my bike and <u>hurt myself</u>.
(다치다)
③ She stayed home <u>by herself</u> all day.
(혼자서)
④ <u>Help yourself</u> to anything on the table.
(자신을 돕다)
⑤ They <u>enjoyed themselves</u> at the beach.
(즐거운 시간을 보내다)

07 밑줄 친 부분이 어법상 틀린 것은?

① <u>All the food looks</u> delicious.
② <u>All the books are</u> on the shelf.
③ <u>Each of the rooms have</u> a window.
④ <u>Both languages are</u> difficult to learn.
⑤ <u>Every student is</u> wearing a backpack.

고난도

08 어법상 올바른 문장의 개수는?

ⓐ Every children are laughing.
ⓑ All the guests arrived on time.
ⓒ We cleaned the house ourselves.
ⓓ Let me introduce my family and me.
ⓔ He chose a blue hat, but I prefer the red one.
ⓕ They have two dogs. One is small, and another is big.

① 1개   ② 2개   ③ 3개
④ 4개   ⑤ 5개

✎ **서술형**

09 〈보기〉에서 알맞은 말을 골라 문장을 완성하시오.
(단, 한 번씩만 쓸 것)

보기	all	both	every

(1) _____ student was excited about the field trip.
(2) _____ of the twins play the piano very well.
(3) _____ the seats in the theater were filled.

10 우리말과 일치하도록 주어진 말을 활용하여 문장을 완성하시오.

(1) 여러분 각자 10분의 발표 시간이 있다. (you, have)

→ _____ _____ _____ ten minutes to give a presentation.

(2) 그 병들은 모두 물로 채워져 있다. (the bottles)

→ _____ _____ filled with water.

11 빈칸에 알맞은 재귀대명사를 써서 문장을 완성하시오.

(1) I want to have some time for _____.

(2) Most people love to talk about
_____.

12 우리말과 일치하도록 주어진 말을 활용하여 문장을 완성하시오.

(1) 그는 기타 치는 법을 스스로 배웠다. (teach)

→ _____ how to play the guitar.

(2) 우리는 놀이동산에서 즐거운 시간을 보냈다. (enjoy)

→ _____ at the amusement park.

13 대화를 읽고, 어법상 틀린 부분을 찾아 바르게 고치시오.

A: What did you receive for your birthday?
B: I received two gifts. One was a sweater, and other was a book.

_____ → _____

14 우리말과 일치하도록 빈칸에 알맞은 말을 쓰시오.

A: You have three sisters, don't you?
B: Yeah, that's right.
A: What do they do?
B: (1) _____ a lawyer, and (2) _____ college students. (한 명은 변호사이고, 나머지는 모두 대학생이야.)

15 그림을 보고, 〈조건〉에 맞게 문장을 완성하시오.

조건 1. she, look at, in the mirror를 활용할 것
　　　 2. 현재진행형을 사용할 것
　　　 3. 총 8단어로 쓸 것

→ _____

16 학생들의 통학 수단을 나타내는 표를 보고 나타낸 문장에서 어법상 **틀린** 부분을 찾아 바르게 고치시오.

Walk	Bus	Bicycle	Others
44%	40%	4%	12%

Some walk to school, and the others take the bus to school.

_____ → _____

17 주어진 문장을 지시에 맞게 바꿔 쓰시오.

<u>Each</u> student has homework to do.

(1) 밑줄 친 부분을 Every로 바꿀 것

→ _____

(2) 밑줄 친 부분을 All로 바꿀 것

→ _____

18 대화를 읽고, 밑줄 친 부분을 어법에 맞게 고치시오.

A: Do you know what? My left foot is bigger than (1) the others.

B: That's strange. (2) Both of my foot are the same size.

(1) _____

(2) _____

[19-20] 다음 글을 읽고, 물음에 답하시오.

Yesterday, I read a story about three dogs. <u>그들 모두는 떠돌이 개였다.</u> One day, a kind couple saw the three dogs on the street and brought (1) (them / themselves) home. Thanks to the couple's love and care, they made (2) (them / themselves) at home in the house. Soon, the house became lively with the sounds of the happy dogs.

19 밑줄 친 우리말과 일치하도록 〈조건〉에 맞게 문장을 완성하시오.

조건 1. all, them, stray dogs를 활용할 것
　　　 2. 총 6단어로 쓸 것

→ _____

20 (1), (2)에서 어법상 맞는 것을 괄호 안에서 골라 각각 쓰시오.

(1) _____

(2) _____

Chapter 09

비교

❶ 원급

동등한 두 대상을 비교할 때 쓰며, 형용사나 부사의 원급을 사용해서 나타낸다.

(1) as + 형용사/부사의 원급 + as: ~만큼 …한/하게

Bob is **as tall as** Charlie. Bob은 Charlie만큼 키가 크다.

Kelly can run **as fast as** Jacob. Kelly는 Jacob만큼 빨리 달릴 수 있다.

(2) not + as + 원급 + as: ~만큼 …하지 않은/않게 (= less + 원급 + than: ~보다 덜 …한/하게)

Mt. Seorak is **not as high as** Mt. Halla. 설악산은 한라산만큼 높지는 않다.

= Mt. Seorak is **less high than** Mt. Halla. 설악산은 한라산보다 덜 높다.

❷ 비교급과 최상급

(1) 비교급

'~보다 더 …한/하게'의 의미로 두 대상을 비교할 때 쓰며, 「비교급 + than」 형태로 나타낸다.

This typhoon is **stronger than** the last one. 이번 태풍은 지난번 것보다 더 강력하다.

My brother is **more diligent than** me. 내 남동생은 나보다 더 부지런하다.

(2) 최상급

'가장 ~한/하게'의 의미로 셋 이상을 비교할 때 쓰며, 「the + 최상급」의 형태로 나타낸다. 최상급 뒤에는 주로 「in + 장소/단체」, 「of + 숫자/기간」 형태로 비교의 범위를 나타낸다.

The Nile is **the longest** river *in* the world. 나일 강은 세계에서 가장 긴 강이다.

This song is **the most popular** *of* the five. 이 곡은 다섯 곡 중에서 가장 인기 있는 곡이다.

(3) 비교급과 최상급 만드는 법

대부분의 경우	+ -er/est	cheap	cheaper	cheapest
-e로 끝나는 경우	+ -r/st	large	larger	largest
-y로 끝나는 경우	y를 i로 고치고 + -er/est	easy	easier	easiest
「단모음 + 단자음」으로 끝나는 경우	자음을 한 번 더 쓰고 + -er/est	big	bigger	biggest
2, 3음절 이상인 경우, -ly로 끝나는 부사	more/most + 원급	difficult slowly	**more** difficult **more** slowly	**most** difficult **most** slowly
불규칙 변화	good/well – **better** – **best** many/much – **more** – **most** far – **farther** – **farthest** (거리)		bad – **worse** – **worst** little – **less** – **least** far – **further** – **furthest** (정도)	

A 괄호 안에서 알맞은 것을 고르시오.

1 The weather today is as (cold, colder) as yesterday.

2 Linda isn't as (old, oldest) as she looks.

3 Susan goes shopping (often, more often) than Emily.

4 That was the (happier, happiest) moment of my life.

5 Thomas is the (good, best) student in the class.

6 My new school is (farther, further) away than my old one.

B 밑줄 친 부분을 어법에 맞게 고치시오.

1 I woke up as <u>earlier</u> as I did yesterday.

2 This book is <u>as not interesting</u> as that one.

3 Soccer is <u>popularer</u> than baseball in my country.

4 He is the <u>funnyest</u> boy in my school.

5 Mike is the <u>most good</u> player on the team.

6 That dress is the <u>most little</u> beautiful one.

C 괄호 안의 말을 이용하여 비교하는 문장을 완성하시오.

1 Sue is _____ than Sarah. (patient)

2 Rick is _____ than my little sister. (young)

3 This watch is the _____ in the shop. (expensive)

4 Walking to the station takes _____ than I thought. (long)

5 Drinking tea is _____ than drinking soda. (healthy)

6 After her nap, she didn't feel as _____ as before. (tired)

7 Mercury is the _____ planet to the Sun. (close)

8 The red dress is the _____ of the three. (pretty)

WRITING FOCUS

A 배열 영작   우리말과 일치하도록 괄호 안의 말을 바르게 배열하시오.

1   Jennifer는 여배우만큼 아름답다. (is, beautiful, as, an, Jennifer, as, actress)

➡ _____

2   나의 형은 나만큼 키가 크지 않다. (brother, I, my, am, as, not, tall, is, as)

➡ _____

3   그녀는 한국에서 가장 유명한 가수이다. (most, is, the, famous, in, she, singer, Korea)

➡ _____

4   Steven은 Chris보다 더 조심스럽게 운전한다. (than, more, Chris, carefully, Steven, drives)

➡ _____

5   그것은 내 인생에서 최악의 순간이었다. (was, moment, the, of, worst, it, my, life)

➡ _____

6   그 공원은 우리가 생각했던 것보다 더 멀리 있다. (the, we, than, park, thought, farther away, is)

➡ _____

B 빈칸 완성   우리말과 일치하도록 괄호 안의 말을 이용하여 빈칸에 알맞은 말을 쓰시오.

1   오늘은 이번 달 중 가장 더운 날이었다. (hot, day)

➡ Today was _____ _____ _____ of the month.

2   Beth는 어제만큼 많이 웃지 않았다. (much)

➡ Beth didn't smile _____ _____ _____ she did yesterday.

3   기말고사는 중간고사보다 더 어려웠다. (difficult)

➡ The final exam was _____ _____ _____ the midterm.

4   룸메이트와 사는 것이 혼자 사는 것보다 더 좋다. (good)

➡ Living with a roommate is _____ _____ living alone.

5   그 식당은 어제보다 덜 붐빈다. (crowded)

➡ The restaurant is _____ _____ _____ it was yesterday.

6   세상에서 가장 위험한 동물은 무엇인가요? (dangerous, animal)

➡ What is _____ _____ _____ _____ in the world?

C 문장 완성 우리말과 일치하도록 괄호 안의 말을 이용하여 문장을 완성하시오.

1 Stewart의 아파트는 Bill의 것보다 더 깨끗하다. (clean)

→ Stewart's apartment _____ Bill's.

2 두 번째 시험은 첫 번째만큼 쉬웠다. (easy, the first one)

→ The second test _____ .

3 내 휴대폰은 네 것만큼 오래되지 않았다. (old, yours)

→ My cellphone is _____ .

4 이 소파는 내 것보다 덜 편안하다. (comfortable, mine)

→ This sofa is _____ .

5 그곳은 미국에서 최고의 대학이다. (good, university, the USA)

→ It is _____ .

6 그것은 내 인생에서 가장 당황스러운 순간이었다. (embarrassing, moment, my life)

→ It was _____ .

D 오류 수정 어법상 틀린 부분을 바르게 고쳐 문장을 다시 쓰시오.

1 Amy is as popular than David. (Amy는 David만큼 인기가 있다.)

→ _____

2 His hair isn't as longer as it was. (그의 머리는 예전만큼 길지 않다.)

→ _____

3 I can run more fast than my brother. (나는 나의 형보다 더 빨리 달릴 수 있다.)

→ _____

4 Talking on the phone is easy than writing a letter. (전화로 이야기하는 것이 편지를 쓰는 것보다 더 쉽다.)

→ _____

5 The math test was most difficult of all tests. (수학 시험이 모든 시험 중에서 가장 어려웠다.)

→ _____

6 Lake Baikal is the most deepest lake in the world. (바이칼호는 세계에서 가장 깊은 호수이다.)

→ _____

UNIT 02 여러 가지 비교 표현

GRAMMAR FOCUS

① 원급을 이용한 표현

as + 원급 + as possible = as + 원급 + as + 주어 + can[could] 가능한 한 ~한/하게	He threw the ball **as far as possible**. = He threw the ball **as far as he could**. 그는 가능한 한 멀리 공을 던졌다.
배수사 + as + 원급 + as ~의 몇 배만큼 …한/하게	The pants are **twice as expensive as** the skirt. 그 바지는 그 치마의 두 배만큼 비싸다.

② 비교급을 이용한 표현

much[even, still, far, a lot] + 비교급 + than ~보다 훨씬 더 ~한/하게	Rob is **much smarter than** Brian. Rob은 Brian보다 훨씬 더 똑똑하다.
비교급 + and + 비교급 점점 더 ~한/하게	Her English is getting **better and better**. 그녀의 영어는 점점 더 나아지고 있다. He got **more and more anxious**. 그는 점점 더 불안해졌다.
the + 비교급 ~, the + 비교급 … 더 ~할수록 더 …하다	**The less** you spend, **the more** you can save. 더 적게 쓸수록 더 많이 저축할 수 있다.

③ 최상급을 이용한 표현

one of the + 최상급 + 복수 명사 가장 ~한 … 중 하나	Bach is **one of the greatest musicians** in history. 바흐는 역사상 가장 위대한 음악가 중 한 명이다.
the + 최상급(+ that) + 주어 + have ever p.p. 지금까지 ~한 것 중 가장 …한	It is **the worst movie (that) I have ever seen**. 그것은 내가 지금까지 본 것 중 최악의 영화이다.
비교급 + than any other + 단수 명사 다른 어떤 ~보다 더 …한	Chris is **taller than any other boy** in the class. = Chris is **the tallest boy** in the class. Chris는 그 반에서 다른 어떤 소년보다 키가 더 크다.

EXERCISE A

괄호 안에서 알맞은 것을 고르시오.

1 Ian goes jogging as often as he (can, possible).

2 My brother ate (two, twice) as much as I did.

3 Cars are (very, much) faster than bicycles.

4 The (less, little) you worry, the happier you'll feel.

5 It was the (great, greatest) service I've ever experienced.

6 He is more famous than any other (actor, actors) in Canada.

밑줄 친 부분을 어법에 맞게 고치시오.

1 Stretch your arms as high as <u>you possible</u>.

2 He smiled as brightly as he <u>can</u>.

3 Your dog is <u>as twice heavy as</u> mine.

4 Helen is much <u>emotional</u> than Tim.

5 The test results were <u>very</u> worse than before.

6 My cat is getting <u>fat and fat</u>.

7 The story is getting <u>more interesting and interesting</u>.

8 The more you move, <u>your heart beats faster</u>.

9 The more you exercise, <u>the little</u> weight you gain.

10 Math is one of the most difficult <u>subject</u> for me.

11 What is the <u>funny</u> movie you've ever seen?

12 The hotel is cheaper than any other <u>hotels</u> in town.

우리말과 일치하도록 괄호 안의 말을 이용하여 문장을 완성하시오.

1 점점 더 많은 사람들이 전기차를 선택하고 있다. (many)

→ _____ _____ _____ people are choosing electric cars.

2 그것은 내가 지금까지 읽어 본 것 중 가장 긴 책이다. (long, book)

→ It is the _____ _____ I've _____ _____ .

3 그 코미디 영화는 내 기분은 훨씬 더 좋게 만들었다. (good)

→ The comedy movie made me feel _____ _____ .

4 날씨가 따뜻할수록 나는 기분이 더 좋다. (warm, good)

→ _____ _____ the weather is, _____ _____ I feel.

5 그들은 그 호텔에서 가장 좋은 방 중 한 곳에 묵었다. (nice, room)

→ They stayed in one of the _____ _____ in the hotel.

6 러시아는 세계에서 다른 어떤 나라보다 더 크다. (country)

→ Russia is larger than any other _____ in the world.

WRITING FOCUS

A 배열 영작   우리말과 일치하도록 괄호 안의 말을 바르게 배열하시오.

1   이 나무는 내 키의 두 배만큼 크다. (as, is, tall, as, I, twice, am)

→ This tree _____ .

2   그녀의 케이크는 내 것보다 훨씬 더 맛있어 보인다. (looks, a, mine, tastier, than, lot)

→ Her cake _____ .

3   그녀는 면접을 보는 동안 점점 더 긴장했다. (nervous, she, got, and, more, more)

→ _____ during the interview.

4   잠을 더 적게 잘수록 나는 더 피곤하다. (the, sleep, I, tired, am, less, the, I, more)

→ _____ , _____ .

5   〈Cats〉는 역사상 가장 유명한 뮤지컬 중 하나이다. (the, famous, in, most, of, musicals, one, history)

→ *Cats* is _____ .

6   보스턴은 내가 가 본 곳 중 가장 아름다운 도시이다. (the, been to, beautiful, most, I've, ever, city)

→ Boston is _____ .

B 빈칸 완성   우리말과 일치하도록 괄호 안의 말을 이용하여 빈칸에 알맞은 말을 쓰시오.

1   시간이 평소의 세 배만큼 오래 걸렸다. (long)

→ It took _____ _____ _____ _____ usual.

2   내 눈꺼풀은 점점 더 무거워지고 있다. (heavy)

→ My eyelids are getting _____ _____ _____ .

3   더 열심히 공부할수록 너는 더 좋은 성적을 받는다. (hard, good, grades)

→ _____ _____ you study, _____ _____ _____ you get.

4   그녀는 자신의 인생에서 최악의 경험 중 하나를 우리에게 말해 주었다. (bad, experience)

→ She told us _____ _____ _____ _____ of her life.

5   Lisa는 내가 지금까지 만났던 학생 중 가장 똑똑하다. (smart, student, meet)

→ Lisa is _____ _____ _____ I have _____ _____ .

6   David는 우리 동아리에서 다른 어떤 남자아이보다 더 키가 크다. (tall, boy)

→ David is _____ _____ _____ _____ _____ in our club.

C 문장 완성   우리말과 일치하도록 괄호 안의 말을 이용하여 문장을 완성하시오.

1 그녀는 한국에서 가장 재능 있는 여배우 중 한 명이다. (talented, actress, in Korea)

→ She is _____ .

2 그것은 내가 지금까지 먹어 본 것 중 최고의 음식이다. (good, food, eat)

→ It is _____ .

3 Nancy는 그 반에서 다른 어떤 학생보다 더 일찍 학교에 온다. (early, student, in the class)

→ Nancy comes to school _____ .

4 그 축구 경기는 점점 더 흥미진진해지고 있다. (get, exciting)

→ The soccer game _____ .

5 네 책가방은 내 것의 두 배만큼 크다. (big, as, mine)

→ Your backpack _____ .

6 더 오래 기다릴수록 그는 더 화가 났다. (long, wait, angry, become)

→ The _____ , the _____ .

D 오류 수정   어법상 **틀린** 부분을 바르게 고쳐 문장을 다시 쓰시오.

1 Diamond is harder than any other stones on the Earth.

→ _____

2 This camera is very better than mine.

→ _____

3 The higher you climb, the farthest you can see.

→ _____

4 This is the warmer welcome I've ever received.

→ _____

5 This car is three as expensive as that one.

→ _____

6 Thanksgiving is one of the biggest holiday in the U.S.

→ _____

[01-03] 빈칸에 들어갈 말로 알맞은 것을 고르시오.

01

Linda can run as _____ as Mina.

① fast   ② fastly
③ faster   ④ fastest
⑤ more faster

02

John is _____ than his brother.

① funny   ② funnier
③ funniest   ④ more funny
⑤ most funny

03

A: What would you recommend on the menu?
B: I recommend the seafood pasta. It is the _____ item at our restaurant.

① popular   ② popularer
③ more popular   ④ popularest
⑤ most popular

04 두 문장의 의미가 같도록 할 때, 빈칸에 들어갈 말이 순서대로 짝지어진 것은?

The book is more interesting than the movie.
= The movie is _____ interesting _____ the book.

① so – as   ② as – not
③ not – as   ④ not – than
⑤ not as – as

05 다음 중 어법상 올바른 것은?

① English is as easier than Chinese.
② We didn't try as harder as they did.
③ Your bag is more heavier than mine.
④ Yesterday was the worst day of my life.
⑤ Science is the difficultest subject for me.

빈출
06 우리말을 영어로 잘못 옮긴 것은?

개는 사람보다 냄새를 훨씬 더 잘 맡을 수 있다.

① Dogs can smell far better than humans.
② Dogs can smell very better than humans.
③ Dogs can smell a lot better than humans.
④ Dogs can smell even better than humans.
⑤ Dogs can smell much better than humans.

고난도
07 어법상 올바른 문장을 모두 고르면?

ⓐ It is getting dark and dark.
ⓑ Roses are more pretty than tulips.
ⓒ This is the worst pie I've ever eaten.
ⓓ The teacher spoke as clearly as possible.
ⓔ He weighs three times as much as his son.
ⓕ It is the most little expensive of all.

① ⓐ, ⓒ   ② ⓐ, ⓓ, ⓔ
③ ⓒ, ⓓ, ⓔ   ④ ⓓ, ⓔ
⑤ ⓓ, ⓔ, ⓕ

08 밑줄 친 부분을 잘못 고친 것은?

ⓐ She left for work as early as she <u>can</u>.
ⓑ Janet is <u>very</u> beautiful than her mother.
ⓒ The higher you climb, the <u>good</u> view you can enjoy.
ⓓ Rome is one of the oldest <u>city</u> in Europe.
ⓔ Alex is <u>tallest</u> than any other boy in the room.

① ⓐ → could
② ⓑ → more
③ ⓒ → best
④ ⓓ → cities
⑤ ⓔ → taller

✏ 서술형

09 빈칸에 들어갈 말을 〈보기〉에서 골라 알맞은 형태로 쓰시오.

보기	large	good	often

(1) I go to the gym as _____ as my brother.
(2) His new song is _____ than his last one.
(3) This is the _____ room in the house.

10 우리말과 일치하도록 주어진 말을 바르게 배열하시오.

(1) 너는 가능한 한 빨리 네 항공편을 예약해야 한다.
(possible, your, book, as, flight, soon, as)
→ You should _____
_____ .

(2) 이 가방이 저것보다 훨씬 더 유용해 보인다.
(lot, than, useful, a, that, more, one)
→ This bag looks _____
_____ .

11 어법상 틀린 부분을 찾아 바르게 고치시오.

(1) The gray car is more older than the black one. (회색 차는 검은색 차보다 더 오래되었다.)

_____ → _____

(2) Jack is youngest person of the three.
(Jack은 셋 중에서 가장 어린 사람이다.)

_____ → _____

12 밑줄 친 우리말과 일치하도록 〈조건〉에 맞게 문장을 완성하시오.

A: Hey, David! How was your weekend?
B: <u>나는 놀이공원에서 가장 즐거운 하루를 보냈어.</u>
A: That sounds fun! I'm glad you had a great time.

> 조건 1. have, enjoyable, day를 활용할 것
> 2. 최상급 표현을 사용할 것

→ _____
at the amusement park.

[13-14] 주어진 문장과 의미가 같도록 괄호 안의 말을 사용하여 문장을 완성하시오.

13

My shoes are not as big as yours. (less)

→ Your shoes are _____ _____
_____ mine.

14

He is the wisest man in the village. (any)

→ He is _____ _____
_____ _____ _____ in
the village.

15 그림을 보고, 주어진 말을 활용하여 문장을 완성하시오.

Smartphone $700 Tablet PC $500 Laptop $1,400

(1) The smartphone is _____
_____ _____ the tablet PC.
(expensive)

(2) The tablet PC is _____ _____
_____ the three. (cheap)

(3) The laptop is _____ _____
_____ _____ the smartphone.
(twice, as)

[16-17] 우리말과 일치하도록 주어진 말을 활용하여 문장을 완성하시오.

16

당신이 더 깊이 잠수할수록 압력이 더 높아진다.
(deep, high)

→ _____ _____ you dive,
_____ _____ the pressure gets.

17

모차르트는 역사상 가장 위대한 작곡가 중 한 명이
다. (great, composer)

→ Mozart is _____ _____ _____
_____ _____ _____ in
history.

18 어법상 <u>틀린</u> 문장 <u>2개</u>를 골라 기호를 쓰고, 틀린 부분을
바르게 고치시오.

ⓐ His math score is much higher than
mine.
ⓑ Surfing is becoming more and more
popular.
ⓒ The few mistakes you make, the better
your grade is.
ⓓ The Sahara Desert is one of the hottest
places in the world.
ⓔ Ms. Taylor is kinder than any other
teachers at the school.

(   ) _____ → _____

(   ) _____ → _____

[19-20] 다음 글을 읽고, 물음에 답하시오.

Last Saturday was the (1) _____ (busy) day of
the week. I had (2) _____ (much) things to do
than usual. But my friends wanted me to go to a
baseball game with them. <u>그것은 내가 지금까지 본
것 중 가장 흥미진진한 경기였다.</u> We had a lot of fun!

19 괄호 안에 주어진 말을 활용하여 빈칸 (1)과 (2)에 알맞은
말을 쓰시오.

(1) _____   (2) _____

20 밑줄 친 우리말과 일치하도록 〈조건〉에 맞게 문장을 완성
하시오.

조건   1. it, exciting, game, see를 활용할 것
2. 줄임말을 쓰지 않을 것
3. 총 10단어로 쓸 것

→ _____
_____

Chapter 10

관계대명사

주격, 소유격 관계대명사

GRAMMAR FOCUS

① 관계대명사의 역할과 쓰임

관계대명사는 접속사와 대명사의 역할을 하며, 관계대명사가 이끄는 절은 형용사절로 앞에 오는 명사(선행사)를 꾸며 준다.

My brother ate *the cookies*. + I made **them**.

→ My brother ate *the cookies* **which** I made.   내 남동생은 내가 만든 쿠키들을 먹었다.
　　　　　　　　　선행사

② 주격 관계대명사

관계대명사절에서 주어 역할을 하며, 선행사에 따라 who, which, that을 쓴다.

사람	who, that	I have a friend. + **She** lives in another country. → I have a friend **who[that]** lives in another country. 나는 다른 나라에 사는 친구가 한 명 있다.
사물, 동물	which, that	The trees are tall. + **They** stand in the park. → The trees **which[that]** stand in the park are tall. 공원에 서 있는 나무들은 키가 크다.

cf. 1. 주격 관계대명사절의 동사는 선행사의 수에 일치시킨다.

Look at *the kids* **who** are playing soccer.   축구하고 있는 아이들을 봐.
　　　　　　　　└ is (×)

2. 「주격 관계대명사 + be동사」는 생략할 수 있다.

The boy (**who is**) talking on the phone is Aron   통화하고 있는 남자아이는 Aron이다.

③ 소유격 관계대명사

소유격 관계대명사는 관계대명사절에서 소유격 역할을 하며, 선행사의 종류에 관계없이 항상 whose를 쓴다.

사람, 사물, 동물	whose	I met a boy. + **His** father is a teacher. → I met a boy **whose** father is a teacher. 나는 아버지가 교사인 한 남자아이를 만났다. The house is my grandmother's. + **Its** roof is green. → The house **whose** roof is green is my grandmother's. 지붕이 녹색인 그 집은 나의 할머니의 집이다.

EXERCISE

A　괄호 안에서 알맞은 것을 고르시오.

1 He is the man (who, which) lives next door.

2 This is a song (who, that) makes me feel happy.

3 I know a boy (who, whose) uncle is a diplomat.

4 She bought earrings (whose, that) are made of gold.

5 We found a house (which, whose) location is convenient.

6 He is writing a novel (which, whose) is about a magic dragon.

EXERCISE
B 우리말과 일치하도록 빈칸에 알맞은 관계대명사를 쓰시오.

1 나는 할인 판매 중인 셔츠 한 장을 샀다.

→ I bought a shirt _____ was on sale.

2 Claire는 나를 잘 이해해주는 친구이다.

→ Claire is a friend _____ understands me well.

3 그는 손잡이가 부러진 여행 가방 하나를 가지고 있다.

→ He has a suitcase _____ handle is broken.

4 그 정원에 핀 꽃들은 아름답다.

→ The flowers _____ bloom in the garden are beautiful.

5 내 이름을 부른 사람은 Johnson 선생님이셨다.

→ The person _____ called my name was Mr. Johnson.

6 자전거를 도난당한 그 소년은 울었다.

→ The boy _____ bike was stolen cried.

EXERCISE
C 두 문장을 관계대명사를 사용하여 한 문장으로 연결하시오.

1 A pilot is a person. He flies an airplane.

→ _____

2 Kate is wearing a backpack. It is full of books.

→ _____

3 I met a girl. Her smile was pretty.

→ _____

4 Andy has a parrot. It has colorful feathers.

→ _____

5 He is the person. He leads the project.

→ _____

6 There is a river near my town. Its water is clear.

→ _____

WRITING FOCUS

A 배열 영작   우리말과 일치하도록 괄호 안의 말을 바르게 배열하시오.

1 그 기자는 그 경주에서 우승한 남자를 인터뷰했다. (man, the, who, race, won, the)

→ The reporter interviewed _____.

2 드론을 날리고 있는 그 남자아이는 신나 보인다. (boy, flying, is, a, who, the, drone)

→ _____ looks excited.

3 Ron은 Iowa에 위치한 한 농장에서 일한다. (is, which, in, located, Iowa)

→ Ron works on a farm _____.

4 그녀는 긴 끈이 달린 지갑 하나를 골랐다. (purse, a, that, a, strap, has, long)

→ She chose _____.

5 Amy는 다리가 부러진 고양이 한 마리를 발견했다. (a, leg, was, cat, whose, broken)

→ Amy found _____.

6 나는 공이 연못에 빠진 한 여자아이를 도와주었다. (fell, a, into, girl, whose, ball, a, pond)

→ I helped _____.

B 빈칸 완성   우리말과 일치하도록 괄호 안의 말과 관계대명사를 이용하여 빈칸에 알맞은 말을 쓰시오.

1 시험에 합격한 그 학생들은 기뻐했다. (pass)

→ The students _____ _____ the exam were happy.

2 경찰은 방 안에 숨어 있던 그 도둑을 발견했다. (hide)

→ The police found the thief _____ _____ _____ inside the room.

3 그는 아픈 아이들을 돕는 한 자선 단체에서 일한다. (help)

→ He works for a charity _____ _____ sick children.

4 나의 아버지는 나에게 내 이름이 새겨진 팔찌를 주셨다. (have)

→ My father gave me a bracelet _____ _____ my name on it.

5 눈이 파란색인 그 소녀는 매우 예쁘다. (eyes)

→ The girl _____ _____ _____ blue is very pretty.

6 이 선물은 생일이 오늘인 한 사람에게 주어질 것이다. (birthday)

→ This gift will be given to a person _____ _____ _____ today.

C 문장 완성　우리말과 일치하도록 괄호 안의 말과 관계대명사를 이용하여 문장을 완성하시오.

1 나는 호주에 사는 친구가 한 명 있다. (a friend, in Australia)

→ I have _____.

2 그는 수상해 보이는 한 남자를 쫓아갔다. (a man, look suspicious)

→ He followed _____.

3 나는 수영장이 있는 체육관을 찾고 있다. (a gym, have, a swimming pool)

→ I am looking for _____.

4 그녀는 선반 위에 있던 책 한 권을 꺼냈다. (a book, on the shelf)

→ She took _____.

5 표지가 가죽으로 만들어진 그 일기장은 내 것이다. (cover, be made of, leather)

→ The diary _____ is mine.

6 나는 변호사가 되는 것이 꿈인 친구가 한 명 있다. (dream, to become a lawyer)

→ I have a friend _____.

D 오류 수정　어법상 틀린 부분을 바르게 고쳐 문장을 다시 쓰시오.

1 She often visits her aunt which lives in Seoul. (그녀는 서울에 사는 이모를 자주 방문한다.)

→ _____

2 I like movies who have happy endings. (나는 행복한 결말이 있는 영화들을 좋아한다.)

→ _____

3 I met a man who speak five languages. (나는 5개 국어를 하는 한 남자를 만났다.)

→ _____

4 Who ate the cookies which was on the table? (누가 식탁 위에 있던 쿠키들을 먹었니?)

→ _____

5 I have a friend which name is the same as mine. (나는 이름이 나와 같은 친구가 한 명 있다.)

→ _____

6 Look at the house that window is broken. (창문이 깨진 집을 봐.)

→ _____

① 목적격 관계대명사

관계대명사절에서 목적어 역할을 하며, 선행사에 따라 who(m), which, that을 쓴다.

사람	**who(m), that**	The girl is my sister. + You met **her**. → The girl **who(m)[that]** you met is my sister. 네가 만난 그 여자아이는 내 여동생이다.
사물, 동물	**which, that**	I found the umbrella. + I lost **it** yesterday. → I found the umbrella **which[that]** I lost yesterday. 나는 어제 잃어버렸던 그 우산을 찾았다.

cf. 1. 목적격 관계대명사가 이끄는 절에 목적어를 중복해서 쓰지 않도록 주의한다.

I found the umbrella **which** I lost **it** yesterday. (×)

2. 목적격 관계대명사는 생략할 수 있다.

Did you read the memo (**that**) I wrote? 너는 내가 쓴 메모를 읽었니?

② 관계대명사 what

선행사를 포함하는 관계대명사로 the thing(s) that[which]으로 바꿔 쓸 수 있으며, '~하는 것'으로 해석한다.
what이 이끄는 절은 명사절로 문장에서 주어, 보어, 목적어 역할을 한다.

What he wants to buy is a nice car. 그가 사고 싶은 것은 멋진 차이다. 〈주어〉

This is **what** I need. 이것은 내가 필요한 것이다. 〈보어〉

Did you hear **what** she just said? 너는 그녀가 방금 말한 것을 들었니? 〈목적어〉

plus 관계대명사 what vs. that

관계대명사 what은 명사절을 이끌어 선행사가 없지만, 관계대명사 that은 형용사절을 이끌어 선행사를 꾸며 준다.

Please show me **what** you bought yesterday. 네가 어제 산 것을 나에게 보여 줘. 〈선행사 없음〉
명사절(~하는 것)

I didn't like *the dress* **that** he bought for me. 나는 그가 나에게 사 준 드레스가 마음에 들지 않았다. 〈선행사 있음〉
형용사절(~하는)

EXERCISE

A 괄호 안에서 알맞은 것을 고르시오.

1 He is the man (who, whom) helped me.

2 The book (whom, which) he wrote is interesting.

3 She is the student (whom, which) everyone likes.

4 I have a question (that, what) I want to ask you.

5 I didn't understand (that, what) the teacher said.

6 All (that, what) I want is a glass of water.

EXERCISE
B   관계대명사 that 또는 what을 써서 문장을 완성하시오.

1 Is this the book _____ you ordered?

2 She reviewed _____ she learned in class.

3 I visited the restaurant _____ my friend recommended.

4 _____ I read in the article was surprising.

5 The car _____ he drives is brand new.

6 I forgot _____ my mom told me in the morning.

7 The dog _____ we adopted from the shelter is very friendly.

8 The movie _____ we watched last night was thrilling.

9 She showed me _____ she bought at the store.

10 Tell me _____ you want for your birthday.

11 The house _____ they live in has a beautiful garden.

12 I can't believe _____ just happened.

EXERCISE
C   괄호 안에 주어진 관계대명사를 사용하여 두 문장을 한 문장으로 연결하시오.

1 She is the girl. Peter likes her so much. (whom)

→ _____

2 This is the song. I heard it on the radio. (which)

→ _____

3 Tell me the thing. You want it for Christmas. (what)

→ _____

4 Jane wore the dress. Her mother made it for her. (which)

→ _____

5 He took out the thing. It was inside the box. (what)

→ _____

6 This is the rule. Every student must follow it. (that)

→ _____

WRITING FOCUS

A 배열 영작   우리말과 일치하도록 괄호 안의 말을 바르게 배열하시오.

1 나는 우리 아빠가 다녔던 학교를 방문했다. (my, the, which, dad, went to, school)

→ I visited _____.

2 내가 좋아하는 그 선생님은 매우 친절하시다. (the, I, teacher, like, whom)

→ _____ is very kind.

3 제가 당신을 위해 해드릴 것이 있나요? (anything, for, can, I, do, that, you)

→ Is there _____?

4 Jack은 항상 그가 약속한 것을 실천한다. (he, what, promises)

→ Jack always does _____.

5 이것은 내가 찾고 있는 것이 아니다. (what, am, I, looking for)

→ This is not _____.

6 그가 찍은 그 사진은 내 주의를 끌었다. (took, the, he, photo)

→ _____ caught my attention.

B 빈칸 완성   우리말과 일치하도록 괄호 안의 말을 이용하여 빈칸에 알맞은 말을 쓰시오.

1 그가 고친 그 컴퓨터는 잘 작동한다. (fix)

→ The computer _____ _____ _____ is working well.

2 나는 우리 엄마가 만드는 음식을 좋아한다. (my mom, make)

→ I like the food _____ _____ _____ _____.

3 네가 먹고 있는 것은 너의 건강에 좋지 않다. (eat)

→ _____ _____ _____ _____ is not good for your health.

4 그녀는 나에게 자신이 짠 목도리를 주었다. (knit)

→ She gave me the scarf _____ _____ _____.

5 내가 도와준 그 남자는 나에게 고마워했다. (help)

→ The man _____ _____ _____ thanked me.

6 그는 여행에 필요한 것들을 샀다. (need)

→ He packed the things _____ _____ _____ for the trip.

C 문장 완성   우리말과 일치하도록 괄호 안의 말을 이용하여 문장을 완성하시오.

1 당신이 필요한 것을 제게 말씀해 주세요. (what, need)

→ Tell me _____ .

2 내가 잃어버린 그 책은 아직 찾지 못했다. (the book, lose)

→ _____ still missing.

3 그 결과는 우리가 기대했던 것이 아니다. (what, expect)

→ The result is not _____ .

4 Nancy는 내가 함께 공부하는 친구이다. (a friend, study with)

→ Nancy _____ .

5 그녀가 만든 샌드위치는 맛있었다. (the sandwiches, make)

→ _____ delicious.

6 그가 말한 것은 모두를 놀라게 했다. (what, say, surprised)

→ _____ everyone.

D 오류 수정   어법상 **틀린** 부분을 바르게 고쳐 문장을 다시 쓰시오.

1 He is the person which I admire. (그는 내가 존경하는 사람이다.)

→ _____

2 I borrowed the book which I wanted to read it. (나는 내가 읽고 싶은 책을 빌렸다.)

→ _____

3 Sue has a brother who she has to take care of him. (Sue는 돌봐야 하는 남동생이 한 명 있다.)

→ _____

4 The glasses that I lost was in the drawer. (내가 잃어버린 그 안경은 서랍 속에 있었다.)

→ _____

5 He told me that he saw last night. (그는 어젯밤에 자신이 본 것을 나에게 말했다.)

→ _____

6 The picture is beautiful that the artist painted. (그 화가가 그린 그림은 아름답다.)

→ _____

ACTUAL TEST

01 빈칸에 들어갈 말이 순서대로 짝지어진 것은?

> • I have a sister _____ is a teacher.
> • There is a bakery _____ sells delicious cakes.

① who – who
② who – which
③ whom – who
④ who – whose
⑤ whose – which

02 빈칸에 들어갈 수 <u>없는</u> 것을 <u>모두</u> 고르면?

> He is the boy _____ I go to school with every day.

① that
② who
③ which
④ whom
⑤ whose

03 밑줄 친 부분을 생략할 수 <u>없는</u> 것은?

① Mike is a friend <u>whom</u> I can trust.
② I like the dress <u>that</u> Emily is wearing.
③ The car <u>which</u> my father drives is silver.
④ Look at the girl <u>who</u> is playing the piano.
⑤ The people <u>that</u> live next door are friendly.

04 밑줄 친 부분의 쓰임이 나머지 넷과 <u>다른</u> 것은?

① The dog <u>that</u> followed us was cute.
② I like movies <u>that</u> have a lot of humor.
③ The computer <u>which</u> I use is very fast.
④ Do you know <u>who</u> is singing that song?
⑤ He works for a company <u>which</u> makes toys.

05 두 문장을 관계대명사를 사용하여 한 문장으로 바르게 바꾼 것은?

> • The girl looks pretty.
> • Her eyes are brown.

① The girl looks pretty that eyes are brown.
② The girl that eyes are brown looks pretty.
③ The girl which eyes are brown looks pretty.
④ The girl whose eyes are brown looks pretty.
⑤ The girl looks pretty whose eyes are brown.

06 우리말을 영어로 바르게 옮긴 것은?

> 나는 그가 내게 말한 것을 믿을 수 없었다.

① I couldn't believe he said to me.
② I couldn't believe that he said to me.
③ I couldn't believe what he said to me.
④ I couldn't believe which he said to me.
⑤ I couldn't believe the thing what he said to me.

07 다음 중 어법상 틀린 문장을 <u>모두</u> 고르면?

① Look at the sign that says, "Stop."
② The boy who backpack is blue is Tom.
③ A rabbit is an animal which has long ears.
④ This is the necklace what my aunt gave me.
⑤ He is a neighbor whom I've known for years.

고난도

08 어법상 올바른 문장을 <u>모두</u> 고르면?

ⓐ I like bags which has a lot of pockets.
ⓑ I lost the watch my dad bought for me.
ⓒ This is the letter that she wrote it to me.
ⓓ He is the soccer player whom I want to meet.
ⓔ The town was beautiful which I saw on TV.
ⓕ I read a news article about a dog that saved a life.

① ⓐ, ⓓ, ⓔ   ② ⓐ, ⓑ, ⓕ
③ ⓑ, ⓒ, ⓔ   ④ ⓑ, ⓓ, ⓕ
⑤ ⓓ, ⓔ, ⓕ

✏️ 서술형

09 〈보기〉에서 알맞은 말을 골라 문장을 완성하시오.

| 보기 | who | which | whose |

(1) I met a musician _____ is very famous.
(2) He is a writer _____ book is a best seller.
(3) These are pictures _____ I took in London.

10 우리말과 일치하도록 주어진 말을 바르게 배열하시오.

(1) 내 옆에 앉아 있던 그 여자는 친절했다.
(who, the, was, woman, sitting, kind, me, was, next to)

→ _____

(2) 우리는 피카소에 의해 그려진 그림을 보았다.
(painting, we, Picasso, saw, a, was, by, which, painted)

→ _____

11 우리말과 일치하도록 〈조건〉에 맞게 문장을 완성하시오.

> 조건   1. 관계대명사 who 또는 which를 사용할 것
>   2. 괄호 안에 주어진 말을 활용할 것

(1) 그는 프랑스에서 유명한 소설가이다.
(a novelist, famous, in France)

→ _____

(2) 나는 집을 청소할 수 있는 로봇을 원한다.
(a robot, the house, can, clean)

→ _____

12 어법상 <u>틀린</u> 부분을 찾아 바르게 고치시오.

(1) Tom has a friend who live in Japan.
(Tom은 일본에 사는 친구가 한 명 있다.)

_____ → _____

(2) He is fixing a bike which chain is broken.
(그는 체인이 고장난 자전거를 고치고 있다.)

_____ → _____

13 주어진 문장과 의미가 같도록 문장을 바꿔 쓰시오.

(1) The temple that we visited was very old.

→ _____
_____ was very old.

(2) The boy who is wearing a cap is my brother.

→ _____
_____ _____ is my brother.

14 대화를 읽고, 어법상 <u>틀린</u> 부분을 찾아 바르게 고치시오.

A: Did you see the laptop at the store?
B: Yes, it was exactly that I wanted, so I decided to buy it.

_____ → _____

15 그림을 보고, 〈조건〉에 맞게 문장을 완성하시오.

조건 1. 관계대명사 who 또는 which를 사용할 것
2. 괄호 안에 주어진 말을 활용할 것
3. 관계대명사절은 현재진행형을 사용할 것

(1) The girl _____

has curly hair. (the candles, blow out)

(2) The cake _____

is heart-shaped. (the man, hold)

16 두 문장을 관계대명사를 사용하여 한 문장으로 바꿔 쓰시오.

(1) I know a café. The café's sandwiches are delicious.

→ _____

(2) He found the scooter. He lost it yesterday.

→ _____

17 우리말과 일치하도록 〈보기〉에서 필요한 단어들만 골라 배열하여 문장을 완성하시오.

(1) 탁자 위에 있는 꽃들은 싱싱해 보인다.

보기 the flowers   that   is   are   fresh
look   looks   on the table

→ _____

(2) 반짝이는 모든 것이 금은 아니다.

보기 that   what   all   is
glitters   not   gold

→ _____

18 어법상 틀린 문장 2개를 골라 기호를 쓰고, 틀린 부분을 바르게 고치시오.

ⓐ John is the nicest man that I know.
ⓑ I want a table which is big and round.
ⓒ He is the teacher I admire the most.
ⓓ The man whose won the race received a medal.
ⓔ I don't like people who makes a lot of noise in public places.

(   ) _____ → _____

(   ) _____ → _____

[19~20] 대화를 읽고, 물음에 답하시오.

A: What's the title of the book (1) (that / what) you read last week? Did you say *An Extraordinary Boy*?

B: Yes, that's right. It is about a boy (2) (who / whose) has *autism. He has special abilities that normal people don't have. 그는 그가 보는 것을 기억할 수 있어.

A: Wow, that's interesting.

B: He is now a lawyer and helps a lot of people. You should read it, too.

*autism 자폐

19 (1), (2)에서 어법상 알맞은 것을 골라 쓰시오.

(1) _____ (2) _____

20 밑줄 친 우리말과 일치하도록 〈조건〉에 맞게 문장을 완성하시오.

조건 1. can, remember, see를 활용할 것
2. 총 6단어로 쓸 것

→ _____

Chapter 11

접속사

❶ 등위접속사

등위접속사는 문법적으로 대등한 단어와 단어, 구와 구, 절과 절을 연결한다. 절과 절을 연결할 때는 접속사 앞에 콤마(,)를 쓴다.

Sam hates peas **and** eggplants.　Sam은 완두콩과 가지를 싫어한다. 〈단어 + 단어〉

I set the alarm **but** didn't hear it.　나는 알람을 맞춰 놓았지만 듣지 못했다. 〈구 + 구〉

Did you go to school by bus **or** on foot?　너는 학교에 버스로 갔니 걸어서 갔니? 〈구 + 구〉

It rained heavily, **so** we stayed indoors.　비가 많이 와서 우리는 실내에 있었다. 〈절 + 절〉

plus 명령문, and ～: …해라, 그러면 ～할 것이다 / 명령문, or ～: …해라, 그렇지 않으면 ～할 것이다

Hurry up, **and** you will be on time.　서둘러, **그러면** 너는 제시간에 도착할 거야.

(= If you hurry up, you will be on time.)

Hurry up, **or** you won't be on time.　서둘러, **그렇지 않으면** 너는 제 시간에 도착하지 못할 거야.

(= If you don't hurry up, you won't be on time.)

❷ 상관접속사

두 개 이상의 단어가 짝을 이루어 쓰이는 접속사로서, 등위접속사와 마찬가지로 문법적으로 대등한 것을 연결한다. 상관접속사가 주어로 쓰인 경우에는 동사의 수 일치에 주의해야 한다.

both A and B A와 B 둘 다	복수 취급	**Both** *my sister* **and** *my brother* **are** tall. 나의 누나와 형 둘 다 키가 크다.
either A or B A나 B 둘 중 하나	동사는 B에 일치	**Either** you **or** *Steve* **has** to give the presentation. 너나 Steve 둘 중 한 명이 발표를 해야 한다.
neither A nor B A도 B도 아닌		**Neither** Todd **nor** *I* **drink** milk. Todd도 나도 우유를 마시지 않는다.
not only A but also B = B as well as A A뿐만 아니라 B도		**Not only** Pam **but also** *her parents* **were** kind to me. = *Her parents* **as well as** Pam **were** kind to me. Pam뿐만 아니라 그녀의 부모님도 나에게 친절했다.

EXERCISE A

괄호 안에서 알맞은 것을 고르시오.

1 Scott (and, so) his family are visiting us next weekend.

2 We can have a picnic in the park (but, or) go to the beach.

3 I rang the doorbell, (but, so) there was no response.

4 My sister had a cold, (or, so) she took some medicine.

5 Eat some food, (and, or) you will get hungry soon.

6 Put on your coat, (and, or) you won't catch a cold.

EXERCISE
B 〈보기〉에서 알맞은 말을 골라 두 문장을 한 문장으로 바꿔 쓰시오. (중복 사용 가능)

보기	and	but	or	so

1 I went to the grocery store to buy milk. I went to the grocery store to buy butter.

→ I went to the grocery store to buy milk _____ butter.

2 These jeans are old. These jeans are comfortable.

→ These jeans are old _____ comfortable.

3 Tom was late for class. His teacher warned him.

→ Tom was late for class, _____ his teacher warned him.

4 Study hard. You will fail the course.

→ Study hard, _____ you will fail the course.

5 Be nice to people. They will be nice to you, too.

→ Be nice to people, _____ they will be nice to you, too.

EXERCISE
C 우리말과 일치하도록 빈칸에 알맞은 말을 쓰시오.

1 그 아파트는 작지만 학교에 가깝다.

→ The apartment is small, _____ it is close to school.

2 Michael은 새로운 도시로 이사를 가서 많은 친구들을 사귀었다.

→ Michael moved to a new city _____ made a lot of friends.

3 당신은 제게 여권과 비자를 둘 다 보여 주셔야 합니다.

→ You have to show me _____ your passport _____ visa.

4 그녀는 그 일을 할 사람으로 Rob 또는 Brian 둘 중 한 명을 선택할 것이다.

→ She will choose _____ Rob _____ Brian for the job.

5 그 뮤지컬은 좋지도 나쁘지도 않았다.

→ The musical was _____ good _____ bad.

6 그 작가는 미국에서뿐만 아니라 유럽에서도 인기가 있다.

→ The writer is popular in Europe _____ _____ _____ in America.

WRITING FOCUS

A 배열 영작 우리말과 일치하도록 괄호 안의 말을 바르게 배열하시오.

1 Amy는 나에게 전화해서 도움을 요청했다. (and, called, for, Amy, asked, me, help)

→ _____

2 비가 내리고 있어서 나는 내 우산을 가져왔다. (raining, so, my, was, I, umbrella, it, brought)

→ _____

3 네 어머니께 전화해, 그렇지 않으면 그분이 걱정하실 거야. (call, be, your, she, mother, will, or, worried)

→ _____

4 그 교습은 유익하지도 재미있지도 않았다. (the, was, neither, lesson, nor, informative, fun)

→ _____

5 나는 스키와 수영을 둘 다 즐긴다. (I, skiing, enjoy, swimming, and, both)

→ _____

6 당신뿐만 아니라 나도 그것에 대한 책임이 있다. (but, I, only, you, also, not, for, am, it, responsible)

→ _____

B 빈칸 완성 우리말과 일치하도록 괄호 안의 말을 이용하여 빈칸에 알맞은 말을 쓰시오.

1 나는 바빠서 Jim에게 전화하는 것을 잊었다. (forget)

→ I was busy, _____ _____ _____ to call Jim.

2 직진하세요, 그러면 경찰서를 찾을 수 있을 거예요. (go straight)

→ _____ _____, _____ you will find the police station.

3 Tim도 나도 그 영화를 좋아하지 않는다. (like)

→ _____ _____ _____ _____ _____ the film.

4 이집트와 수단 둘 다 아프리카에 있다. (Egypt, Sudan)

→ _____ _____ _____ _____ _____ in Africa.

5 그는 거만할 뿐 아니라 이기적이다. (arrogant, selfish)

→ He is _____ _____ _____ _____ _____ _____.

6 Peter나 그의 아이들이 저녁 식사 후에 설거지를 한다. (wash)

→ _____ Peter _____ his children _____ the dishes after dinner.

C 문장 완성 우리말과 일치하도록 괄호 안의 말을 이용하여 문장을 완성하시오.

1 나는 매우 화가 나서 그에게 소리쳤다. (shout at)

→ I was very angry, _____.

2 그는 영어를 잘 못하지만 그것을 이해할 수는 있다. (can, understand, it)

→ He can't speak English well, _____.

3 빨리 일해, 그러면 너는 그것을 오늘 끝낼 수 있어. (can, finish)

→ Work quickly, _____ today.

4 서둘러, 그렇지 않으면 너는 네 비행기를 놓칠 거야. (will, miss, flight)

→ Hurry up, _____.

5 당신은 그곳까지 가는데 버스나 지하철 중 하나를 탈 수 있다. (the bus, the subway)

→ You can take _____ to get there.

6 돈뿐만 아니라 시간도 귀중하다. (not, also, money, time)

→ _____ valuable.

D 오류 수정 어법상 **틀린** 부분을 바르게 고쳐 문장을 다시 쓰시오.

1 That dress is beautiful and expensive. (저 원피스는 아름답지만 비싸다.)

→ _____

2 I usually read books or watching movies on Saturday. (나는 토요일에 주로 책을 읽거나 영화를 본다.)

→ _____

3 Drink some water, and you will get thirsty. (물을 좀 마셔, 그렇지 않으면 너는 목이 마를 거야.)

→ _____

4 Susan eats neither meat or fish. (Susan은 고기도 생선도 먹지 않는다.)

→ _____

5 Both Fred and Luke is good at math. (Fred와 Luke 둘 다 수학을 잘한다.)

→ _____

6 Her sisters as well as Jane is intelligent. (Jane뿐만 아니라 그녀의 자매들도 똑똑하다.)

→ _____

❶ 시간, 조건을 나타내는 접속사

when	~할 때	**When** I entered the classroom, no one was there. 내가 교실에 들어갔을 때, 거기에는 아무도 없었다.
while	~하는 동안	I burned my finger **while** I was cooking. 나는 요리를 하는 동안 손가락을 데었다.
as	~할 때, ~하면서	He saw her **as** he was getting off the bus. 그는 버스에서 내리면서 그녀를 보았다.
until, till	~할 때까지	Let's wait **until** the books are on sale. 책을 할인할 때까지 기다리자.
before	~ 전에	He watched some TV **before** he went to bed. 그는 자러 가기 전에 TV를 조금 보았다.
after	~ 후에	**After** we finished shopping, we had dinner. 우리는 쇼핑을 마친 후에 저녁을 먹었다.
if	(만일) ~한다면	**If** we *don't leave* now, we will be late. = **Unless** we *leave* now, we will be late.
unless	(만일) ~하지 않으면	우리는 지금 떠나지 않으면 늦을 것이다.

plus 시간, 조건의 부사절에서는 현재시제로 미래를 나타낸다.

I will call you **when** I *get* home. 내가 집에 도착하면 너에게 전화할게.

If Kelly *comes*, I will ask her the question. Kelly가 온다면 나는 그녀에게 그 질문을 할 것이다.

❷ 이유, 양보를 나타내는 접속사

because, as, since	~ 때문에	The match was canceled **because** it rained. 그 시합은 비가 왔기 때문에 취소되었다. **Since** it was Sunday, he stayed in bed longer. 일요일이었기 때문에 그는 침대에 더 오래 있었다.
although, though, even though	비록 ~이지만	**Although** he failed, he was not discouraged. 그는 실패했지만 낙담하지 않았다.

plus because of(~ 때문에) 다음에는 절이 아닌 명사(구)가 온다.

The match was canceled **because of** *the rain*. 그 시합은 비 때문에 취소되었다.

❸ 결과를 나타내는 접속사

so + 형용사/부사 + that...	너무 ~해서 …하다	Toby was **so** *tired* **that** he fell asleep in class. Toby는 너무 피곤해서 수업 중에 잠이 들었다.
such (a/an) + 형용사 + 명사 + that...		It was **such** *a hot day* **that** we went swimming. 너무 더운 날이라서 우리는 수영을 하러 갔다.

plus 목적을 나타내는 so that ~ 구문과 혼동하지 않도록 주의한다.

He studied *hard* **so that** he could pass the exam. 그는 시험에 합격**하기 위해서** 열심히 공부했다. 〈목적〉

He studied **so** *hard* **that** he could pass the exam. 그는 **매우** 열심히 공부**해서** 시험에 합격할 수 있었다. 〈결과〉

EXERCISE A

괄호 안에서 알맞은 것을 고르시오.

1 We were having dinner (when, because) Christina got home.

2 I will ride my bike to school (if, unless) it is not raining.

3 (Although, While) Jim was working in the yard, he hurt his back.

4 (When, Unless) you have a driver's license, you must not drive.

5 The room was (so, such) dirty that Andy decided to clean it up.

6 I will go out to play after I (finish, will finish) my homework.

EXERCISE B

〈보기〉에서 알맞은 접속사를 골라 문장을 완성하시오. (단, 한 번씩만 쓸 것)

보기	although	because	that	unless	until

1 _____ you put the ice in the freezer, it will melt.

2 Helen has to take the bus _____ she lives far away from school.

3 I had to wait _____ the bank opened.

4 _____ the house is old, it is well maintained.

5 We were so hungry _____ we ordered a lot of food.

EXERCISE C

밑줄 친 부분을 어법에 맞게 고치시오.

1 You can't go to the university <u>if</u> you finish high school.

2 <u>Because</u> Sarah was sick, she didn't miss school.

3 It was <u>so</u> an expensive car that he couldn't buy it.

4 My father wants to retire when he <u>will be</u> 60 years old.

5 If he <u>will miss</u> the bus, he will be late for work.

6 The music was <u>loud so</u> that we couldn't hear each other.

7 He was disappointed <u>because of</u> the results weren't good.

WRITING FOCUS

A 배열 영작   우리말과 일치하도록 괄호 안의 말을 바르게 배열하시오.

1 그는 차를 몰고 가면서 우리에게 손을 흔들었다. (as, away, he, drove)

→ _____, he waved at us.

2 우리가 저녁 식사를 하는 동안 전기가 나갔다. (we, having, while, were, dinner)

→ _____, the electricity went off.

3 Phil이 10분 안에 오지 않으면 내가 그에게 전화할게. (Phil, in, come, if, ten, doesn't, minutes)

→ _____, I will call him.

4 그는 자신의 등록금을 내야 했기 때문에 돈을 좀 빌렸다. (he, his, pay, because, tuition, had to)

→ He borrowed some money _____.

5 내 방은 내가 2시간 동안 청소를 했지만 여전히 지저분해 보인다. (it, for, although, cleaned, two, I, hours)

→ My room still looks messy _____.

6 Lisa는 너무 천천히 걸어서 제시간에 도착할 수 없었다. (she, so, that, couldn't, slowly, arrive)

→ Lisa walked _____ on time.

B 빈칸 완성   우리말과 일치하도록 괄호 안의 말을 이용하여 빈칸에 알맞은 말을 쓰시오.

1 자기 전에 따뜻한 우유를 좀 마시는 게 어때? (sleep)

→ Why don't you drink some warm milk _____ _____ _____?

2 Jane이 일찍 도착한다면 우리는 저녁을 먹으러 나갈 것이다. (arrive)

→ _____ _____ _____ early, we will go out to dinner.

3 그는 곤경에 처해 있었지만 나의 도움을 거절했다. (in trouble)

→ _____ _____ _____ _____ _____, he refused my help.

4 그녀는 감기에 걸렸기 때문에 일찍 떠났다. (have a cold)

→ _____ _____ _____ _____ _____, she left early.

5 그는 교직에서 은퇴할 때까지 3년의 시간이 있다. (retire)

→ He has three years _____ _____ _____ from teaching.

6 그가 너무 빨리 말했기 때문에 나는 그의 말을 이해할 수 없었다. (fast, understand)

→ He spoke _____ _____ _____ I _____ _____ him.

C 문장 전환 〈보기〉에서 알맞은 접속사를 골라 두 문장을 한 문장으로 바꿔 쓰시오. (단, 한 번씩만 쓸 것)

| 보기 | because | even though | so ~ that... | such ~ that... | until |

1 He can speak English. He lived in Canada for three years.

→ _____

2 Traffic was heavy. She made it to work on time.

→ _____

3 I will wait for you. You are ready.

→ _____

4 His accent was very strong. I couldn't understand him.

→ _____

5 It was very good weather. We went on a picnic.

→ _____

D 오류 수정 어법상 **틀린** 부분을 바르게 고쳐 문장을 다시 쓰시오.

1 Can you wait until I will call your name? (제가 당신의 이름을 부를 때까지 기다려 주시겠습니까?)

→ _____

2 Let's go to the zoo another time unless you're tired. (네가 피곤하다면 동물원은 다음에 가자.)

→ _____

3 The coffee was good so that I had two cups. (그 커피는 너무 맛있어서 나는 두 잔을 마셨다.)

→ _____

4 Ali did well on the test because he didn't study hard. (Ali는 열심히 공부하지 않았지만 시험을 잘 봤다.)

→ _____

5 If it will rain tomorrow, we won't go to the park. (내일 비가 온다면 우리는 공원에 가지 않을 것이다.)

→ _____

6 Mary got angry because of her vase was broken. (Mary는 그녀의 꽃병이 깨져서 화가 났다.)

→ _____

① 명사절 접속사 that

that이 이끄는 명사절은 '~라는 것'으로 해석되며, 문장에서 주어, 보어, 목적어 역할을 한다. that절이 주어로 쓰인 경우에는 주로 가주어 it으로 대신하고 that절은 문장 뒤로 보낸다.

주어	**That** he is 83 years old is surprising. = **It** is surprising **that** he is 83 years old. 가주어 / 진주어
보어	The problem is **that** we don't have time.
목적어	I think (**that**) the book is interesting. *명사절이 목적어일 때 that은 생략 가능

그가 83세라는 것은 놀랍다.

문제는 우리가 시간이 없다는 것이다.

나는 그 책이 흥미롭다고 생각한다.

cf. 명사절 접속사 that vs. 관계대명사 that

접속사 that은 주어, 보어, 목적어 역할을 하는 명사절을 이끌며, 뒤에는 완전한 문장이 온다. 관계대명사 that은 선행사를 수식하는 형용사절을 이끌며, 뒤에는 주어나 목적어가 빠진 불완전한 문장이 온다.

I think **that he is a reliable person**. 나는 그가 신뢰할 만한 사람이라고 생각한다. 〈명사절 접속사 that〉
I liked *the movie* **that we watched yesterday**. 나는 우리가 어제 본 영화가 좋았다. 〈관계대명사 that〉

② 간접의문문

간접의문문은 의문문이 다른 문장 안에 쓰인 것으로, 의문사 또는 if[whether]가 접속사 역할을 한다.

의문사가 있는 경우 「의문사 + 주어 + 동사」	Tell me. + *Why are you* angry? → Tell me **why you are** angry. 네가 왜 화가 났는지 나에게 말해 줘.
의문사가 주어인 경우 「의문사 + 동사」	Do you know? + *Who lives* next door? → Do you know **who lives** next door? 너는 누가 옆집에 사는지 알고 있니?
의문사가 없는 경우 「if/whether + 주어 + 동사」	I don't know. + *Did he receive* my letter. → I don't know **if[whether]** he received my letter. 나는 그가 내 편지를 받았는지 모르겠다.

cf. 주어 자리에는 if를 쓰지 않는다.

Whether he likes me is not important. 그가 나를 좋아하는지는 중요하지 않다.
⌊→ If (×)

EXERCISE
A   다음 문장을 밑줄 친 부분에 주의하여 우리말로 해석하시오.

1 It is true <u>that</u> the Earth is round.

→ _____

2 The problem is <u>that</u> I lost my cellphone.

→ _____

3 Doctors say <u>that</u> getting enough sleep is important.

→ _____

EXERCISE
B   다음 두 문장을 한 문장으로 바꿔 쓰시오.

1 I don't understand. + Why is she always late?

→ _____

2 Do you know? + How long does it take to get there?

→ _____

3 He didn't tell me. + What happened last night?

→ _____

4 I wonder. + Can you help me with my homework?

→ _____

EXERCISE
C   우리말과 일치하도록 빈칸에 알맞은 말을 쓰시오.

1 그가 그 해일에서 살아남은 것은 기적이었다.

→ It was a miracle _____ he survived the tsunami.

2 나는 우리가 그 형편없는 서비스에 대해 불만을 제기해야 한다고 생각한다.

→ I think _____ we should complain about the poor service.

3 가장 가까운 슈퍼마켓이 어디인지 알려 주시겠어요?

→ Could you tell me _____ the nearest supermarket is?

4 그가 올지 안 올지는 불확실하다.

→ _____ he will come or not is uncertain.

WRITING FOCUS

A 배열 영작 우리말과 일치하도록 괄호 안의 말을 바르게 배열하시오.

1 진실은 내가 그를 믿지 않는다는 것이다. (the, is, that, truth, don't, I, him, trust)

→ _____

2 나는 고기를 먹는 것이 필요하다고 생각한다. (I, that, necessary, meat, think, is, eating)

→ _____

3 나는 그녀에게 어떻게 연락할 수 있는지 궁금하다. (contact, I, her, can, wonder, how, I)

→ _____

4 그는 어디에 자신의 차를 주차했는지를 잊어버렸다. (his, he, where, parked, forgot, he, car)

→ _____

5 그 판사는 그녀가 유죄인지를 결정해야 한다. (if, the, guilty, judge, she, has to, is, decide)

→ _____

6 그가 일자리를 구할 수 있을지는 확실하지 않다. (is, a, can, certain, job, whether, he, get, not)

→ _____

B 빈칸 완성 우리말과 일치하도록 괄호 안의 말을 이용하여 빈칸에 알맞은 말을 쓰시오.

1 문제는 내가 내 지갑을 집에 두고 왔다는 것이다. (the problem)

→ _____ _____ _____ _____ I left my wallet at home.

2 우리는 그가 정직하다고 믿는다. (honest)

→ We believe _____ _____ _____ _____.

3 David가 그 노트북을 훔쳤다는 것은 놀라운 일이다. (surprising)

→ _____ _____ _____ _____ David stole the laptop.

4 당신은 그 상점이 언제 문을 닫는지 알고 있습니까? (the shop, close)

→ Do you know _____ _____ _____ _____ ?

5 제가 다음에 무엇을 해야 할지 알려 주세요. (should, do)

→ Let me know _____ _____ _____ _____ next.

6 우리는 그 정보가 사실인지 아닌지 확인해야 한다. (the information, true)

→ We should check _____ _____ _____ _____ _____ or not.

C 문장 완성   우리말과 일치하도록 괄호 안의 말을 이용하여 문장을 완성하시오.

1 우리 팀이 그 경기에 진 것은 실망스러웠다. (it, disappointing)

→ _____ our team lost the game.

2 중요한 것은 우리가 건강하다는 것이다. (healthy)

→ The important thing _____ .

3 나는 누가 이 곡을 썼는지 궁금하다. (write, this song)

→ I wonder _____ .

4 나는 그녀가 몇 살인지 모른다. (old)

→ I don't know _____ .

5 나는 내일 일찍 일어날 수 있을지 잘 모르겠다. (can, get up early)

→ I'm not sure _____ tomorrow.

6 그는 그 온라인 강좌를 들을지 말지 결정하지 못했다. (will, take the online course)

→ He hasn't decided _____ or not.

D 오류 수정   어법상 틀린 부분을 바르게 고쳐 문장을 다시 쓰시오.

1 They believe if he will win the election. (그들은 그가 당선될 거라고 믿는다.)

→ _____

2 What she was interested in me was surprising. (그녀가 내게 관심이 있었다는 것은 놀라웠다.)

→ _____

3 I don't remember what is her name. (나는 그녀의 이름이 무엇인지 기억나지 않는다.)

→ _____

4 Do you know where did he go on vacation? (너는 그가 어디로 휴가를 갔는지 아니?)

→ _____

5 I don't know who the water spilled on the carpet. (나는 누가 카펫에 물을 쏟았는지 모른다.)

→ _____

6 If the rumor is true or not is uncertain. (그 소문이 사실인지 아닌지는 불확실하다.)

→ _____

ACTUAL TEST

01 빈칸에 들어갈 말로 알맞은 것은?

> Take this medicine, _____ you will get better.

① and ② but ③ or
④ so ⑤ if

02 빈칸에 들어갈 말이 순서대로 짝지어진 것은?

> • _____ I was scared, I went on the roller coaster.
> • We walked there _____ it wasn't too far.

① As – when
② If – though
③ When – until
④ Because – since
⑤ Although – because

03 다음 중 어법상 올바른 것은?

① Both Tom and Jane was late.
② Neither she nor I speaks English.
③ Either Mom or Dad has the car keys.
④ Not only he but also his brother are tall.
⑤ Tom as well as I enjoy playing basketball.

_{빈출}
04 밑줄 친 접속사의 쓰임이 어색한 것은?

① I fell asleep while I was reading a book.
② As I had nothing to say, I remained silent.
③ He made a plan before he started to work.
④ You can't drive if you have a driver's license.
⑤ Although she was shy, she made some new friends at school.

05 우리말을 영어로 바르게 옮긴 것은?

> 택시를 타지 않는다면 우리는 늦을 거야.

① We'll be late if we take a taxi.
② We'll be late unless we take a taxi.
③ We'll be late if we won't take a taxi.
④ We'll be late unless we will take a taxi.
⑤ We'll be late unless we don't take a taxi.

06 우리말과 일치하도록 주어진 말을 배열할 때, 네 번째로 오는 단어는?

> 그 영화는 너무 슬퍼서 모두가 울었다.
> (everyone, the, was, sad, so, that, cried, movie)

① so ② sad ③ that
④ cried ⑤ everyone

07 밑줄 친 부분의 쓰임이 나머지 넷과 다른 것은?

① I heard that he is from Scotland.
② He told us a story that is inspiring.
③ I think that you should get some rest.
④ It is surprising that she drew the picture.
⑤ The truth is that we can't change the past.

08 두 문장을 한 문장으로 바꿔 쓸 때 빈칸에 알맞은 것은?

> I wonder. + Whose bag is this?
> → I wonder _____.

① this is whose bag
② whose bag is this
③ whose bag this is
④ if whose bag is this
⑤ whether whose bag this is

09 빈칸에 공통으로 들어갈 말은?

- I asked her _____ she was coming.
- _____ it will rain tomorrow is uncertain.

① if[If]　　　　　　② as[As]
③ that[That]　　　　④ when[When]
⑤ whether[Whether]

고난도

10 어법상 올바른 문장의 개수는?

ⓐ Be quiet, and she will wake up.
ⓑ Her name is either Susan or Emily.
ⓒ I am not sure where is the gas station.
ⓓ Do you know who made these cookies?
ⓔ I was tired so that I wanted to take a nap.
ⓕ It was such cold that we stayed indoors.

① 1개　　　　② 2개　　　　③ 3개
④ 4개　　　　⑤ 5개

✏ 서술형

11 두 문장의 의미가 같도록 빈칸에 알맞은 말을 쓰시오.

(1) If you exercise regularly, you will be healthy.

→ _____ _____, _____ you will be healthy.

(2) If you don't take an umbrella, you will get wet.

→ _____ _____ _____, _____ you will get wet.

12 우리말과 일치하도록 필요한 단어들만 골라 배열하여 문장을 완성하시오.

(1) 우리는 프랑스와 스페인 둘 다 여행했다.
(traveled, we, to, both, France, Spain, or, and)

→ _____

(2) 헬렌켈러는 볼 수도 들을 수도 없었다.
(Helen Keller, neither, could, or, nor, and, see, hear, not)

→ _____

13 각 상자에서 필요한 말을 하나씩 골라 문장을 완성하시오.

if	I just ate breakfast
that	you aren't busy
although	the Earth is round

(1) It is true _____.
(2) Let's go to the movies _____.
(3) I feel hungry _____.

14 어법상 틀린 부분을 찾아 바르게 고치시오.

(1) After I will finish my homework, I will watch TV.

_____ → _____

(2) If she will have time tomorrow, she will go shopping.

_____ → _____

15 그림을 보고, 〈조건〉에 맞게 대화를 완성하시오.

> 조건 1. tight, can't, move를 포함할 것
> 2. so ~ that 구문을 사용할 것

A: How do they fit?
B: These jeans are _____
_____ _____ _____
_____ _____ properly.

16 우리말과 일치하도록 주어진 말을 바르게 배열하시오.

(1) 그 책은 너무 재미있어서 나는 그것을 하루 만에 다 읽었다. (was, I, the, it, so, that, interesting, book, finished)

→ _____
in just a day.

(2) 너무 바쁜 하루여서 나는 점심을 걸렀다. (it, such, that, busy, a, skipped, day, I, lunch, was)

→ _____

17 주어진 문장과 의미가 같도록 빈칸에 알맞은 말을 쓰시오.

> If you don't run, you will miss the train.

→ _____ you run, you will miss the train.

18 다음 표를 보고, 〈조건〉에 맞게 문장을 완성하시오.

	Sora	Jiho	Mina
I live in...	Seoul	Busan	Seoul
I like...	chicken	chicken	beef
I'm good at...	English	math	math

> 조건 상관접속사와 표에 주어진 표현을 활용할 것

(1) _____ Sora _____ Mina
_____ in Busan.

(2) _____ Sora _____ Jiho
_____ chicken.

(3) _____ _____ Jiho _____
_____ Mina _____ good at
math.

19 다음 의문문을 간접의문문으로 바꿔 문장을 완성하시오.

(1) When will the class begin?

→ Do you know _____.

(2) What happened yesterday?

→ Tell me _____.

(3) Does he have a sister?

→ I wonder _____.

20 빈칸에 공통으로 들어갈 접속사를 쓰시오.

- _____ we were walking to the park, we saw a beautiful sunset.
- _____ the elevator broke down, I had to take the stairs.

Chapter
12

가정법

GRAMMAR FOCUS

❶ 가정법 과거

가정법 과거는 현재 사실과 반대되거나 실현 가능성이 희박한 일을 가정할 때 쓴다. If절의 동사를 과거형으로 써서 나타내며, '(만일) ~라면, …할 텐데'의 의미이다.

If + 주어 + 동사의 과거형 ~, (만일) ~라면,	주어 + 조동사의 과거형 + 동사원형 …할 텐데
If I **were** you, 내가 너라면	I **would go** to the doctor. 병원에 가 볼 텐데.
If I **had** some money, 내게 돈이 좀 있다면	I **could buy** her a present. 그녀에게 선물을 사 줄 수 있을 텐데.

cf. 가정법 과거에서 if절의 be동사는 주어의 인칭과 수에 관계없이 were를 주로 사용한다.

❷ 가정법 과거의 문장 전환

가정법 과거는 이유의 접속사(because, as 등)를 사용해서 직설법 현재로 바꿔 쓸 수 있다. 가정법 과거를 직설법 현재로 바꿀 때는 긍정은 부정으로, 부정은 긍정으로 바꾸고, 시제를 현재로 바꾼다.

If I **knew** the answer, I **could tell** you. 내가 답을 안다면, 네게 말해 줄 수 있을 텐데.
→ As I **don't know** the answer, I **can't tell** you.

If he **weren't** busy, he **would come** with us. 그가 바쁘지 않다면, 우리와 함께 갈 텐데.
→ As he **is** busy, he **won't come** with us.

❸ 조건문 vs. 가정법 과거

조건문은 현재나 미래에 실현 가능성이 있을 때 쓰고, 가정법 과거는 현재 사실과 반대되거나 실현 가능성이 희박한 일을 가정할 때 쓴다.

조건문	If I **go** to Paris, I **will** **visit** the Eiffel Tower. 내가 파리에 가면, 에펠탑을 방문할 것이다. 〈파리에 갈 가능성이 있음〉
가정법 과거	If I **went** to Paris, I **would** **visit** the Eiffel Tower. 내가 파리에 간다면, 에펠탑을 방문할 텐데. 〈파리에 갈 가능성이 희박함〉

EXERCISE A

괄호 안에서 알맞은 것을 고르시오.

1 If it (rains, rained) tomorrow, we will cancel the picnic.

2 If I (have, had) a brother or a sister, I would be less bored.

3 If I (am, were) you, I would not make that decision.

4 Get some rest if you (feel, felt) sick.

5 I (will, would) let you know if I find your watch.

6 If traffic were not heavy, we (can, could) get there on time.

EXERCISE
B

우리말과 일치하도록 〈보기〉에서 알맞은 말을 골라 문장을 완성하시오. (필요시 형태를 바꿀 것)

보기	be	fall	take	use	wear

1 제가 당신의 컴퓨터를 사용해도 될까요?

→ Will it be okay if I _____ your computer?

2 우리가 택시를 탄다면, 집에 더 일찍 도착할 텐데.

→ If we _____ a taxi, we would get home earlier.

3 네가 조심하지 않으면, 넘어질 수도 있어.

→ If you don't watch out, you can _____.

4 이곳에 다른 누군가가 있다면 나는 무섭지 않을 텐데.

→ I wouldn't be scared if there _____ someone else here.

5 내가 너라면, 이렇게 추운 날씨에 그 재킷을 입지 않을 텐데.

→ If I were you, I wouldn't _____ that jacket in this cold weather.

EXERCISE
C

두 문장의 의미가 같도록 빈칸에 알맞은 말을 쓰시오.

1 As I am so busy, I won't go on vacation.

→ If I _____ so busy, I _____ _____ on vacation.

2 As he doesn't have a car, he doesn't drive to work.

→ If he _____ a car, he _____ _____ to work.

3 I won't play outside because I have homework.

→ If I _____ _____ homework, I _____ _____ outside.

4 As it isn't sunny, we won't go to the beach.

→ If it _____ sunny, we _____ _____ to the beach.

5 As we don't live closer, we can't see each other more often.

→ If we _____ closer, we _____ _____ each other more often.

6 As she speaks too fast, I can't understand her.

→ If she _____ _____ too fast, I _____ _____ her.

WRITING FOCUS

A 배열 영작   우리말과 일치하도록 괄호 안의 말을 바르게 배열하시오.

1 네가 코트를 입지 않는다면, 추울 거야. (don't, you, be, will, wear, you, a, cold, coat)

→ If _____ , _____ .

2 나에게 돈이 좀 있다면, 그 가방을 살 텐데. (had, I, buy, some, the, money, would, I, bag)

→ If _____ , _____ .

3 비가 오고 있지 않다면, 우리는 산책을 하러 갈 텐데. (we, weren't, go, it, raining, would, for a walk)

→ If _____ , _____ .

4 내가 너라면, 진실을 말할 텐데. (tell, I, you, would, the, were, I, truth)

→ If _____ , _____ .

5 너에게 백만 달러가 있다면 무엇을 할 거니? (you, if, had, you, a million dollars, do, would)

→ What _____ ?

6 그에게 열쇠가 있다면 문을 열 수 있을 텐데. (unlock, if, the key, could, he, had, the door)

→ He _____ .

B 빈칸 완성   우리말과 일치하도록 괄호 안의 말을 이용하여 가정법 문장을 완성하시오.

1 네가 지금 출발한다면, 제시간에 도착할 수 있을 텐데. (leave, arrive)

→ If you _____ now, you _____ _____ on time.

2 우리가 버스를 탄다면, 더 저렴할 텐데. (take, cheaper)

→ If we _____ the bus, it _____ _____ _____ .

3 나에게 내 친구들이 없다면, 외로움을 느낄 텐데. (have, feel)

→ If I _____ _____ my friends, I _____ _____ lonely.

4 내가 너라면, 패스트푸드를 너무 많이 먹지 않을 텐데. (be, eat)

→ If I _____ you, I _____ _____ too much fast food.

5 그가 재즈에 대해 더 잘 안다면, 이 콘서트를 즐길 텐데. (know, enjoy)

→ If he _____ more about jazz, he _____ _____ this concert.

6 네가 더 일찍 일어난다면, 공부할 시간이 더 많을 텐데. (get up, have)

→ If you _____ _____ earlier, you _____ _____ more time to study.

C 문장 전환   두 문장의 의미가 같도록 빈칸에 알맞은 말을 쓰시오.

1 As it is so cold, we can't go out today.

→ If it _____ so cold, we _____ _____ out today.

2 As she doesn't like meat, she won't eat the steak.

→ If she _____ meat, she _____ _____ the steak.

3 As he is sick, he can't go skiing.

→ If he _____ sick, he _____ _____ skiing.

4 My uncle lives abroad, so I don't see him often.

→ If my uncle _____ _____ abroad, I _____ _____ him often.

5 I can't call her because I don't have her phone number.

→ If I _____ her phone number, I _____ _____ her.

6 You can't drive a car because you aren't old enough.

→ If you _____ old enough, you _____ _____ a car.

D 오류 수정   밑줄 친 부분을 바르게 고쳐 문장을 다시 쓰시오.

1 If it snowed tomorrow, we will make a snowman.

→ _____

2 If I were taller, I can be a basketball player.

→ _____

3 Where will you like to live if you could choose?

→ _____

4 If the shoes are cheaper, I could buy them.

→ _____

5 If you bought today, you can get a 20% discount.

→ _____

6 If we don't have the map, we would be lost.

→ _____

I wish 가정법 과거, as if 가정법 과거
GRAMMAR FOCUS

❶ I wish 가정법 과거

현재 사실에 반대되는 소망이나 이룰 수 없는 일에 대한 아쉬움을 표현할 때 쓴다. 「I wish + 주어 + 동사의 과거형」
형태로 쓰고, '~라면 좋을 텐데'로 해석한다.

I wish I **were** good at English. 내가 영어를 잘하면 좋을 텐데.

→ I'm sorry that I **am not** good at English.

I wish I **had** a big family like you. 나에게 너처럼 대가족이 있다면 좋을 텐데.

→ I'm sorry that I **don't have** a big family like you.

I wish I **could see** you tomorrow. 내가 내일 너를 볼 수 있으면 좋을 텐데.

→ I'm sorry that I **can't see** you tomorrow.

I wish my grandparents **didn't live** far away. 나의 조부모님이 멀리 떨어져 사시지 않으면 좋을 텐데.

→ I'm sorry that my grandparents **live** far away.

❷ as if 가정법 과거

실제로는 그렇지 않지만 그런 것처럼 가정할 때 쓴다. 「as if + 주어 + 동사의 과거형」 형태로 쓰고, '마치 ~한 것처럼'으로
해석한다.

They look **as if** they **were** sisters. 그들은 마치 자매인 것처럼 보인다.

→ In fact, they **aren't** sisters.

Aiden talks **as if** he **knew** everything. Aiden은 마치 모든 것을 아는 것처럼 말한다.

→ In fact, Aiden **doesn't know** everything.

> **plus** as if 가정법 과거는 주절의 시제와 관계없이, 주절과 동일한 시점의 일을 반대로 가정할 때 쓴다.
>
> He **acts** as if he **were** my friend. 그는 마치 내 친구인 것처럼 행동한다.
> He **acted** as if he **were** my friend. 그는 마치 내 친구인 것처럼 행동했다.

A 괄호 안에서 알맞은 것을 고르시오.

1 I wish I (am, were) a movie star.

2 I wish I (had, have) a sister.

3 I wish I (can, could) speak every language.

4 I wish I (didn't doesn't) have to study for exams.

5 She talks as if she (is, were) my mother.

6 Live each day as if today (is, were) your last.

7 I feel as if I (am, were) dreaming.

8 He smiled as if he (were, weren't) sad.

EXERCISE B

두 문장의 의미가 같도록 빈칸에 알맞은 말을 쓰시오.

1 I wish I had my own bedroom.

→ I'm sorry that I _____ _____ my own bedroom.

2 I wish I could play the piano.

→ I'm sorry that I _____ _____ the piano.

3 I wish my hair were longer.

→ I'm sorry that my hair _____ _____ longer.

4 She talks as if she didn't know anything.

→ In fact, she _____ something.

5 He talks as if he lived in New York

→ In fact, he _____ _____ in New York.

6 She sings as if she were a famous singer.

→ In fact, she _____ _____ a famous singer.

EXERCISE C

우리말과 일치하도록 빈칸에 알맞은 말을 써서 가정법 문장을 완성하시오.

1 오늘이 내 생일이면 좋을 텐데.

→ I wish today _____ my birthday.

2 나에게 새 컴퓨터가 있으면 좋을 텐데.

→ I wish I _____ a new computer.

3 내 부모님이 나를 더 잘 이해해주시면 좋을 텐데.

→ I wish my parents _____ me better.

4 오늘은 미세먼지가 없으면 좋을 텐데.

→ I wish there _____ no fine dust today.

5 John은 마치 그 문제를 풀 수 있는 것처럼 말한다.

→ John talks as if he _____ _____ the problem.

6 그녀는 내가 마치 아이인 것처럼 대한다.

→ She treats me as if I _____ a child.

WRITING FOCUS

A 배열 영작　우리말과 일치하도록 괄호 안의 말을 바르게 배열하시오.

1　오늘이 휴일이면 좋을 텐데. (were, a, today, holiday)

→ I wish _____.

2　시험이 없다면 좋을 텐데. (were, no, there, tests)

→ I wish _____.

3　나에게 좋은 집이 있으면 좋을 텐데. (I, nice, had, a, house)

→ I wish _____.

4　네가 네 친구들에게 더 친절하면 좋을 텐데. (you, nicer, friends, to, were, your)

→ I wish _____.

5　그는 마치 걱정이 없는 것처럼 행동한다. (if, he, as, no, had, worries)

→ He acts _____.

6　그녀는 마치 그에 대해 신경 쓰지 않는 것처럼 말한다. (care about, she, didn't, if, him, as)

→ She talks _____.

B 빈칸 완성　우리말과 일치하도록 빈칸을 채워 가정법 문장을 완성하시오.

1　내가 유명한 배우라면 좋을 텐데. (be)

→ I wish _____ _____ a famous actor.

2　내게 더 자신감이 있다면 좋을 텐데. (have)

→ I wish _____ _____ more confidence.

3　내가 가족과 함께 시간을 더 보내면 좋을 텐데. (spend)

→ I wish _____ _____ more time with my family.

4　세상에 범죄가 없다면 좋을 텐데. (there)

→ I wish _____ _____ no crime in the world.

5　그녀는 마치 모델인 것처럼 걷는다. (be)

→ She walks as if she _____ a model.

6　나는 마치 날고 있는 것 같은 기분이 든다. (flying)

→ I feel as if I _____ _____.

C 문장 전환   두 문장의 의미가 같도록 빈칸에 알맞은 말을 쓰시오.

1 I'm sorry that the sky is not clear.

→ I wish _____ .

2 I'm sorry that I don't have more free time.

→ I wish _____ .

3 I'm sorry that I can't play a musical instrument.

→ I wish _____ .

4 In fact, she isn't my best friend.

→ She talks as if _____ .

5 In fact, he isn't always happy.

→ He acts as if _____ .

6 In fact, they don't understand the situation.

→ They talk as if _____ .

D 오류 수정   어법상 **틀린** 부분을 바르게 고쳐 문장을 다시 쓰시오.

1 I wish every day is Sunday.

→ _____

2 I wish I can sing better.

→ _____

3 I wish there are no wars in the world.

→ _____

4 I wish my grandparents are still alive.

→ _____

5 She spends money as if she is a billionaire.

→ _____

6 I feel as if I am walking on a cloud.

→ _____

ACTUAL TEST

[01-02] 빈칸에 들어갈 말로 알맞은 것은?

01

If he _____ English, he could get the job.

① spoke
② speak
③ speaks
④ will speak
⑤ has spoken

02

I wish I _____ like a bird.

① will fly
② can fly
③ could fly
④ have flown
⑤ am flying

03 두 문장의 의미가 같도록 할 때, 빈칸에 알맞은 것은?

He talks to me as if he were the boss.
→ In fact, he _____ the boss.

① is
② were
③ is not
④ were not
⑤ hasn't been

04 어법상 틀린 부분을 바르게 고친 것은?

Peter stays up late every day. If he didn't stay up late, he will feel less tired.

① stays → stayed
② didn't → doesn't
③ didn't stay → stayed
④ will → would
⑤ less → more

05 주어진 문장을 가정법으로 바르게 바꾼 것은?

I'm sorry that I have homework today.

① I wish I had homework today.
② I wish I have homework today.
③ I wish I don't have homework today.
④ I wish I didn't have homework today.
⑤ I wish I won't have homework today.

06 우리말을 영어로 옮길 때 쓰이지 <u>않는</u> 단어는?

그녀는 마치 나를 낯선 사람처럼 대한다.

① as
② if
③ am
④ treats
⑤ a stranger

빈출 고난도

07 두 문장의 의미가 서로 <u>다른</u> 것은?

① As he is sick, he can't go skiing.
 = If he weren't sick, he could go skiing.
② If I wore glasses, I could see clearly.
 = As I don't wear glasses, I can't see clearly.
③ If the sofa weren't too big, I would buy it.
 = The sofa was too big, so I didn't buy it.
④ The soup is salty, so it doesn't taste good.
 = If the soup weren't salty, it would taste good.
⑤ If we had a map, we could find the way.
 = We can't find the way because we don't have a map.

고난도

08 밑줄 친 부분이 **틀린** 것을 **모두** 고르면?

① Brian wishes he <u>had</u> a pet dog.

② She acts as if she <u>were</u> a princess.

③ If I had more time, I <u>traveled</u> a lot.

④ I wouldn't buy that car if I <u>were</u> you.

⑤ If it weren't cold, I <u>will wear</u> a new skirt.

11 우리말과 일치하도록 〈보기〉에서 필요한 단어들만 골라 배열하여 문장을 완성하시오.

(1) 내 개가 말을 할 수 있으면 좋을 텐데.

보기	I	my	wish	can	dog
	could	talk	talks		

→ _____

(2) Sue는 마치 발레리나인 것처럼 춤을 춘다.

보기	Sue	she	were	ballerina
	as	if	is	dances	a

→ _____

✏ 서술형

09 우리말과 일치하도록 빈칸에 알맞은 말을 쓰시오.

(1) 그가 더 젊다면, 어떤 일이든 할 수 있을 텐데.

→ If he _____ younger, he _____
_____ anything.

(2) 그녀에게 가족이 있다면, 외롭지 않을 텐데.

→ If she _____ a family, she _____
_____ _____ lonely.

[12-14] 어법상 **틀린** 부분을 찾아 바르게 고치시오.

12

My grandmother passed away ten years
ago. If she were alive today, she is 99 years
old!

_____ → _____

13

My phone's battery dies so quickly. I wish
it has a longer battery life.

_____ → _____

10 주어진 말을 바르게 배열하여 문장을 완성하시오.

you, wishes, had, what, magic lamp, make,
you, a, would

→ If _____,
_____ ?

14

The flowers look as if they are real, but they
aren't.

_____ → _____

15 그림을 보고, 〈조건〉에 맞게 문장을 완성하시오.

> 조건 1. have, a yacht, sail을 활용할 것
>   2. 가정법 과거를 사용할 것

→ If I _____, I _____
   around the world.

[16-17] 직설법 문장은 가정법으로, 가정법 문장은 직설법으로 바꿔 쓰시오.

16

As I don't have a car, I can't drive you home.

→ If I _____ a car, I _____ _____ you home.

17

If he were careful, he wouldn't make so many mistakes.

→ As he _____ _____ careful, he _____ many mistakes.

18 주어진 문장과 의미가 같도록 문장을 완성하시오.

(1) I'm sorry that I don't live closer to my school.

→ I wish _____.

(2) In fact, she can't go anywhere in the world.

→ She talks as if _____
   in the world.

19 대화를 읽고, 어법상 틀린 부분 2개를 찾아 바르게 고치시오.

A: What will you do if you met your favorite singer?
B: If I met my favorite singer, I asked him for his autograph on my guitar.

(1) _____ → _____
(2) _____ → _____

20 빈칸에 알맞은 말을 써서 대화를 완성하시오.

A: What would you like to change about your school?
B: I wish there _____ a bigger playground and a nice cafeteria.

+ Memo

최신개정판

문법을 알면 **영작**이 쉽다!

Grammar Plus Writing

전지원 ┃ 박혜영

WORKBOOK

중등 내신 · 서술형 시험 완벽 대비

2

- 중등 필수 영문법을 쉽고 간결하게 설명
- 영작 집중 훈련으로 기초를 탄탄히
- 최신 서술형 연습문제로 실전 대비

DARAKWON

Grammar +Plus Writing

WORKBOOK

2

⊘ Answer Key p.39

A
GRAMMAR

〈보기〉에서 알맞은 말을 골라 문장을 완성하시오. (현재시제를 사용할 것)

| 보기 | bark | be | feel | rain |
| | sleep | smell | turn | work |

1 My cat _____ on my bed.

2 The dog _____ at strangers.

3 Nurses _____ at a hospital.

4 It _____ a lot in the rainforest.

5 You _____ my best friend.

6 The sunlight _____ warm on my back.

7 The milk went bad. It _____ sour.

8 At sunset, the sky _____ red.

B
WRITING

주어진 말을 바르게 배열하여 문장을 완성하시오.

1 the Earth / around the Sun / moves

→ _____

2 study / the students / in the classroom

→ _____

3 they / my relatives / are

→ _____

4 became / her son / a professor

→ _____

5 sounds / this song / familiar

→ _____

⊘ Answer Key p.39

A GRAMMAR

다음 문장을 〈보기〉와 같이 바꿔 쓰시오.

| 보기 | She gave her sister a gift.
→ She gave a gift to her sister.

1 Jack showed us his photo album.

→ _____

2 Mary sent me a Christmas card.

→ _____

3 He made his daughter a sandwich.

→ _____

4 The boy asked his teacher many questions.

→ _____

B WRITING

주어진 말을 바르게 배열하여 문장을 완성하시오.

1 drives / my uncle / a bus / in the city

→ _____

2 science / she / at a high school / teaches

→ _____

3 us / he / a funny joke / told

→ _____

4 lent / to / Andy / his car / his brother

→ _____

5 my parents / a new laptop / me / bought / for

→ _____

⊘ Answer Key p.39

A GRAMMAR

괄호 안의 말을 알맞은 형태로 바꿔 문장을 완성하시오.

1 Music makes me _____. (happy)

2 I want you _____ our book club. (join)

3 She had her son _____ some milk. (buy)

4 They named their son _____. (Andrew)

5 I heard someone _____ for help. (shout)

6 The air conditioner keeps the room _____. (cool)

7 My mom told me _____ my room. (clean)

8 The coach made the players _____ their muscles. (stretch)

9 Tom asked me _____ the remote control. (bring)

10 We watched the man _____ magic tricks. (perform)

B WRITING

밑줄 친 부분을 바르게 고쳐 문장을 다시 쓰시오.

1 I found the class <u>interestingly</u>.

→ _____

2 They elected him <u>as CEO</u>.

→ _____

3 The museum doesn't allow visitors <u>bring</u> their pets inside.

→ _____

4 I had the repairman <u>to fix</u> my computer.

→ _____

5 She felt the wind <u>blew</u> through her hair.

→ _____

현재, 과거, 미래시제

A
GRAMMAR

괄호 안에서 알맞은 것을 고르시오.

1 My family (move, moved) to the U.S. in 2008.

2 We usually (watch, will watch) a movie every Sunday.

3 I (call, will call) you later in the afternoon.

4 Fire (produces, produced) heat and light.

5 She (goes, is going) to meet her friend tomorrow.

6 He (travels, traveled) to Europe last summer.

7 He (is, will be) back from his trip soon.

8 She (bought, will buy) a new car a few days ago.

9 The human body (needs, needed) food for energy.

10 They are going (visit, to visit) the art museum next week.

B
WRITING

우리말과 일치하도록 괄호 안의 말을 이용하여 문장을 완성하시오.

1 밤에는 하늘이 어둡다. (the sky, dark)

→ _____ at night.

2 Tina는 지난 주말에 마라톤을 했다. (run a marathon)

→ _____ last weekend.

3 우리는 내일 동물원에 갈 예정이다. (go to the zoo)

→ We're _____ tomorrow.

4 그는 병원에서 간호사로 일한다. (as a nurse)

→ _____ at a hospital.

5 점심시간이 다 됐네. 나는 샌드위치를 먹어야겠어. (have a sandwich)

→ It's around lunchtime. _____.

⊘ Answer Key p.39

A

GRAMMAR

괄호 안에서 알맞은 것을 고르시오.

1 It (snows, is snowing) outside. Let's make a snowman.

2 I (study, was studying) for my final exams last night.

3 I (want, am wanting) a glass of orange juice.

4 She (is living, was living) in Paris at that time.

5 They (are leaving, were leaving) for L.A. tomorrow.

6 He (takes, was taking) a shower when the doorbell rang.

7 Look! A lot of people (wait, are waiting) in line at that restaurant.

8 This book (is belonging, belongs) to Jeremy.

9 My dad (is cooking, was cooking) dinner in the kitchen now.

10 They (go, are going) shopping later today.

B

WRITING

주어진 말과 진행형을 사용하여 문장을 완성하시오.

1 David / drive / to work / now

→ _____

2 she / walk / her dog / along the river / then

→ _____

3 my cousins / visit / me / next weekend

→ _____

4 Brian / talk / on the phone / at the moment

→ _____

5 they / camp / in the woods / during the storm

→ _____

A
GRAMMAR

괄호 안의 말을 이용하여 현재완료 문장을 완성하시오. (부정문은 줄임말을 사용할 것)

1 I _____ that museum twice. (visit)

2 _____ a shooting star? (you, ever, see)

3 Chris _____ abroad before. (never, travel)

4 They _____ home from their trip. (just, arrive)

5 I _____ dinner, so I'm not hungry. (already, have)

6 Janet _____ her homework yet. (not, finish)

7 I _____ in this city for five years. (live)

8 Steve _____ many friends since he joined the club. (make)

9 He _____ to the gym, so he is not here right now. (go)

10 _____ their lost puppy? (they, find)

B
WRITING

우리말과 일치하도록 괄호 안의 말과 현재완료를 이용하여 문장을 완성하시오.

1 우리는 이미 집을 청소했다. (already, clean, the house)

→ We _____.

2 나는 한 번도 유명인을 만나 본 적이 없다. (meet, never, a celebrity)

→ I _____.

3 누군가 내 우산을 가져가 버렸다. (take, umbrella)

→ Somebody _____.

4 그들은 어린 시절부터 친구였다. (friends, childhood)

→ They _____.

5 나는 파리에 두 번 가 본 적이 있다. (Paris, twice)

→ I _____.

⊘ Answer Key p.40

A
GRAMMAR

괄호 안에서 알맞은 것을 고르시오.

1 Jane (can, may) run fast. She is the fastest in the class.

2 He (can, could) read and write when he was five years old.

3 They (can, will be) able to attend the meeting tomorrow.

4 Bob won first prize. He (may, must) be very happy.

5 They (may, must) be stuck in traffic, but I am not sure.

6 He (must, cannot) be Chinese. He has a Korean passport.

7 She (may, may not) know the answer to that question. Let's ask her.

8 The librarian said, "You (may, must) borrow up to five books at a time."

9 (Could, May) you please wait for me outside?

10 (Will, May) I have your attention, please?

B
WRITING

밑줄 친 부분을 어법에 맞게 고쳐 문장을 다시 쓰시오.

1 She can <u>speaks</u> multiple languages fluently.

→ _____

2 You may <u>using</u> my laptop if you need it.

→ _____

3 They <u>can</u> win against their rival yesterday.

→ _____

4 The bus <u>doesn't may</u> arrive for a long time.

→ _____

5 We will <u>can</u> finish the project by tomorrow.

→ _____

02 의무, 충고, 과거의 습관

⊘ Answer Key p.40

A
GRAMMAR

괄호 안에서 알맞은 것을 고르시오.

1 You (must, used to) wear a seatbelt in the car.

2 In Korea, people (must not, don't have to) smoke in restaurants.

3 She (has better, had better) take some medicine for her headache.

4 You (should, would) brush your teeth after meals.

5 You (must not, don't have to) bring anything. Everything is ready.

6 Last week, I (must, had to) study for an important exam.

7 I (used to, would) live in Paris before I moved here.

8 We (may, ought to) respect others' opinions.

9 When I was little, I (must, would) watch cartoons on Sunday mornings.

10 You (had better not, had not better) drive above the speed limit.

B
WRITING

우리말과 일치하도록 괄호 안의 말과 조동사를 이용하여 문장을 완성하시오.

1 관람객들은 미술관에서 작품들을 만져서는 안 된다. (visitors, touch, the artwork)

→ _____ in the gallery.

2 악천후로 인해 그들은 여행을 취소해야 했다. (cancel, the trip)

→ _____ due to bad weather.

3 이곳에는 제과점이 있었지만, 지금 그곳은 약국이다. (there, a bakery)

→ _____ here, but now it's a pharmacy.

4 우리는 일주일 동안은 식료품을 살 필요가 없다. (buy, groceries)

→ _____ for a week.

5 너는 집에 가는 마지막 버스를 놓치지 않는 것이 좋겠다. (miss, the last bus)

→ _____ home.

to부정사의 명사적 용법

⊘ Answer Key p.40

A
GRAMMAR

〈보기〉에서 알맞은 말을 골라 to부정사를 사용하여 문장을 완성하시오.

|보기|	win	spend	solve	start
	eat	say	buy	lock

1 _____ no is hard for him.

2 He hopes _____ more time with his family.

3 I have no idea how _____ this problem.

4 His plan is _____ his own business next year.

5 It is safe _____ the doors and windows at night.

6 I can't decide where _____ lunch today.

7 Her dream is _____ an Olympic medal.

8 I don't know what _____ as a gift for my friend.

B
WRITING

주어진 말을 바르게 배열하여 문장을 완성하시오.

1 impossible / is / get there / it / 20 minutes / to / within

→ _____

2 is / her / on Broadway / to / dream / perform

→ _____

3 my / study / want / parents / me / medicine / to

→ _____

4 money / they / to / for a vacation / need / save

→ _____

5 grandfather / *baduk* / my / me / how / taught / to / play

→ _____

02 to부정사의 형용사적 용법

⊘ Answer Key p.40

A
GRAMMAR

괄호 안에서 알맞은 것을 고르시오.

1 I have a lot of homework to (do, doing) today.

2 Brian wrapped a gift (gave, to give) to his mom.

3 They rented an apartment to (live, live in).

4 I would like (something hot, hot something) to drink.

5 I have some (books interesting, interesting books) to read.

6 We need (smart someone, someone smart) to do the job.

7 Jenny picked up a pen to (write on, write with).

8 The boy wanted a new toy to (play, play with).

9 She is always looking for different sports to (play, play with).

10 We have (nothing more, more nothing) to discuss today.

B
WRITING

우리말과 일치하도록 괄호 안의 말과 to부정사를 이용하여 문장을 완성하시오.

1 나는 비행 중에 읽을 잡지 한 권을 샀다. (a magazine)

→ I bought _____ during the flight.

2 이 방에는 앉을 의자가 많지 않다. (many chairs)

→ There aren't _____ in this room.

3 나는 이번 주말에 특별히 할 일이 없다. (special, nothing)

→ I have _____ this weekend.

4 그는 이야기할 친구 몇 명이 필요하다. (some friends)

→ He needs _____.

5 나는 내 졸업식 날 입을 멋진 것을 원한다. (nice, something)

→ I want _____ on my graduation day.

⊘ Answer Key p.40

A
GRAMMAR

다음 문장을 〈보기〉와 같이 to부정사를 이용하여 바꿔 쓰시오.

| 보기 | I want to buy a new car, so I am saving money.
→ I am saving money <u>to buy a new car</u>.

1 Julia grew up, and she is now a famous singer.

→ Julia grew up _____ .

2 I was pleased because I found my lost smartphone.

→ I was pleased _____ .

3 He was so tired that he couldn't focus on his work.

→ He was _____ .

4 The weather was so cold that it could freeze the lake.

→ The weather was _____ .

B
WRITING

주어진 말을 바르게 배열하여 문장을 완성하시오.

1 takes notes / remember / he / important / to / information

→ _____

2 Kate / nice / to / must / friends / be / have / so many

→ _____

3 hard / his joke / understand / is / to

→ _____

4 she / to / ride / too / was / short / the roller coaster

→ _____

5 the noise / enough / wake up / was / to / the baby / loud

→ _____

⊘ Answer Key p.41

A

GRAMMAR

괄호 안에서 알맞은 것을 고르시오.

1 There are not enough chairs for (us, we) to sit on.

2 It is nice (for, of) you to open the door hold for me.

3 We decided (to not accept, not to accept) his offer.

4 It was wise (for, of) him to apologize for his mistake.

5 The water was too cold (for, of) me to swim in.

6 Mom told us (not touch, not to touch) the hot stove.

7 It is necessary (for, of) leaders to communicate effectively.

8 It is rude (for, of) them to talk loudly during the movie.

9 Be careful (to break not, not to break) the eggs.

10 It's not easy (for, of) me to memorize people's names.

B

WRITING

어법상 틀린 부분을 바르게 고쳐 문장을 다시 쓰시오.

1 There are many things of us to enjoy in New York City.

→ _____

2 He woke up early to not miss the train.

→ _____

3 It was stupid for him to leave the window open.

→ _____

4 It is difficult of me to cook without a recipe.

→ _____

5 She promised to not tell anyone about the surprise party.

→ _____

⊘ Answer Key p.41

CHAPTER 05

동명사

A GRAMMAR

〈보기〉에서 알맞은 말을 골라 동명사를 사용하여 문장을 완성하시오.

보기	bake	build	drink	find
	play	spill	talk	feel

1 _____ loudly in public places is not polite.

2 Her favorite activity is _____ cupcakes.

3 The kids enjoy _____ board games together.

4 I'm so sorry for _____ coffee on your shirt.

5 The workers are busy _____ a new house.

6 I feel like _____ a glass of water right now.

7 We had difficulty _____ a parking spot downtown.

8 Mary couldn't help _____ nervous before the big exam.

B WRITING

우리말과 일치하도록 괄호 안의 말과 동명사를 이용하여 문장을 완성하시오.

1 그녀는 밖에 나가는 것을 좋아하지 않는다. (like, go outside)

→ _____

2 책을 읽는 것은 즐겁다. (read books, enjoyable)

→ _____

3 그들은 쉬지 않고 일했다. (work, without, take a break)

→ _____

4 John은 TV를 보는 데 너무 많은 시간을 쓴다. (too much time, watch TV)

→ _____

5 그들은 휴가 가는 것을 고대하고 있다. (go on vacation)

→ _____

동명사 vs. to부정사

⊘ Answer Key p.41

A
GRAMMAR

괄호 안에서 알맞은 것을 <u>모두</u> 고르시오.

1 I enjoy (learning, to learn) new languages.

2 We expect (arriving, to arrive) there on time.

3 Mike learned (swimming, to swim) last summer.

4 My sister promised (keeping, to keep) the secret.

5 I finished (reading, to read) the novel last night.

6 He gave up (searching, to search) for the lost keys.

7 I will start (saving, to save) money for my vacation.

8 I remember (meeting, to meet) him a few years ago.

9 She tried to avoid (answering, to answer) my questions.

10 The ice cream has all melted. I forgot (putting, to put) it in the freezer.

B
WRITING

어법상 틀린 부분을 바르게 고쳐 문장을 다시 쓰시오.

1 Do you mind to turn on the air conditioner?

→ _____

2 We decided taking the train instead of flying.

→ _____

3 After a long walk, they stopped getting some rest.

→ _____

4 Remember turning off the light before you leave.

→ _____

5 I'll never forget to visit that beautiful place.

→ _____

UNIT 01 현재분사와 과거분사

Answer Key p.41

A GRAMMAR

괄호 안의 말을 알맞은 형태로 바꿔 문장을 완성하시오.

1 The _____ player is resting on the grass. (injure)

2 The night sky was filled with _____ stars. (shine)

3 The cats _____ their toys are so cute. (chase)

4 The band _____ the music performed well. (play)

5 The car _____ outside belongs to my neighbor. (park)

6 This is a picture _____ by Vincent van Gogh. (paint)

7 The man _____ at us is our tour guide. (wave)

8 Do you know the boy _____ the blue jacket? (wear)

9 The _____ computer is now working well. (repair)

10 Susan found the vase _____ on the floor. (break)

B WRITING

밑줄 친 부분을 바르게 고쳐 문장을 다시 쓰시오.

1 The mechanic is fixing the <u>damage</u> car.

→ _____

2 The <u>bark</u> dog kept me awake all night.

→ _____

3 We saw a hot-air balloon <u>flew</u> in the sky.

→ _____

4 She printed the pictures <u>take</u> in Hawaii.

→ _____

5 There are many trains <u>leave</u> for Busan.

→ _____

02 주의해야 할 분사

⊘ Answer Key p.41

A
GRAMMAR

괄호 안에서 알맞은 것을 고르시오.

1 Jane is (interesting, interested) in art.

2 Taking a warm bath is (relaxing, relaxed).

3 The roller coaster ride was so (exciting, excited).

4 I was (shocking, shocked) to hear the news.

5 The meal on the plane was (satisfying, satisfied).

6 The book was (boring, bored) and made me sleepy.

7 He was (annoying, annoyed) because of the loud music.

8 It was such a (tiring, tired) day, so I went to bed early.

9 People were (disappointing, disappointed) with the concert.

10 Emily felt (embarrassing, embarrassed) when she fell over on the ice.

B
WRITING

어법상 틀린 부분을 바르게 고쳐 문장을 다시 쓰시오.

1 She was depress after her cat's death.

→ _____

2 My son was excite about getting on a plane.

→ _____

3 The lecture was informative but bore.

→ _____

4 He was surprise when he saw the police car.

→ _____

5 His snoring is very annoy.

→ _____

UNIT 01 능동태와 수동태

⊘ Answer Key p.42

A

괄호 안에서 알맞은 것을 고르시오.

1 The gardener (waters, is watered) the flowers.

2 The students (taught, are taught) by Ms. Green.

3 The book (wrote, was written) by a famous author.

4 The team (won, was won) the championship last night.

5 The thief (caught, was caught) by the police.

6 The children are (playing, played) in the park.

7 The song (composed, was composed) by Mozart.

8 The chairman will (make, be made) the decision.

9 The movie (directed, was directed) by Steven Spielberg.

10 The dishes will (wash, be washed) by my dad after dinner.

B

WRITING

주어진 말을 바르게 배열하여 문장을 완성하시오.

1 loved / the book / children / is / by

→ _____

2 the meals / by / are / cooked / the chef

→ _____

3 the gift / the clerk / wrapped / by / was

→ _____

4 broken / the windows / by / were / the storm

→ _____

5 my father / the broken chair / be / will / by / fixed

→ _____

02 수동태의 여러 가지 형태

⊘ Answer Key p.42

A
GRAMMAR

다음 문장을 〈보기〉와 같이 바꿔 쓰시오.

> | 보기 | The company does not make the goods.
> → The goods are not made by the company.

1 Mr. Wilson did not answer the question.

→ _____

2 Did Jane Austen write the novel?

→ _____

3 The team may do the new project.

→ _____

4 Children should not watch the movie.

→ _____

B
WRITING

우리말과 일치하도록 괄호 안의 말을 이용하여 수동태 문장을 완성하시오.

1 그 실수는 내가 저지르지 않았다. (the mistake, make)

→ _____

2 이 벽은 그가 페인트칠을 했니? (this wall, paint)

→ _____

3 그 앱은 누구나 이용할 수 있다. (the app, use, anyone, can)

→ _____

4 교실은 학생들에 의해 청소되나요? (the classroom, clean, students)

→ _____

5 초콜릿은 개들이 먹어서는 안 된다. (chocolate, dogs, must, eat)

→ _____

03 주의해야 할 수동태

⊘ Answer Key p.42

A
GRAMMAR

괄호 안에서 알맞은 것을 고르시오.

1 She is worried (about, by) her exam.

2 I am tired (of, in) hearing his excuses.

3 The sofa is covered (from, with) a blanket.

4 The ship is made (of, from) steel.

5 The beach is known (for, about) its white sand.

6 The tour bus is filled (of, with) tourists from Japan.

7 This small village is not known (to, by) many people.

8 I wasn't satisfied (from, with) their response to my request.

9 The book was written (in, by) Spanish.

10 My smartphone was stolen (at, by) the gym.

B
WRITING

우리말과 일치하도록 괄호 안의 말을 이용하여 문장을 완성하시오.

1 나는 클래식 음악에 관심이 있다. (interest, classical music)

→ _____

2 그 가게는 꽃 향기로 가득 차 있다. (the shop, fill, the scent of flowers)

→ _____

3 그 주스는 사과와 당근으로 만들어진다. (the juice, make, apples and carrots)

→ _____

4 그 운동회는 매년 개최된다. (the sporting event, hold, every year)

→ _____

5 그 집은 20년 전에 지어졌다. (the house, build, twenty years ago)

→ _____

⊘ Answer Key p.42

A
GRAMMAR

괄호 안에서 알맞은 것을 고르시오.

1 Janet bought a new sofa. She loves (it, one).

2 I don't have a pen. Can I borrow (it, one)?

3 Emma lost her gloves. She has to buy new (one, ones).

4 Some people like to rest in their free time. (Other, Others) like to travel.

5 I have three pens. One is red, (another, the other) is blue, and the other is black.

6 There are two swimming pools. One is indoors, and (another, the other) is outdoors.

7 (Every, All) student is in the auditorium for graduation.

8 (Every, All) the furniture belongs to her.

9 Each of us (has, have) a book to read.

10 Both of my grandparents (enjoy, enjoys) traveling.

B
WRITING

어법상 틀린 부분을 바르게 고쳐 문장을 다시 쓰시오.

1 I needed a new pencil case, so I bought it online.

→ I needed a new pencil case, so _____.

2 I have two fish. One is gold, and other is black.

→ I have two fish. _____.

3 All the food taste delicious.

→ All the food _____.

4 Every flowers in the garden has bloomed.

→ _____ has bloomed.

5 Each of the cars need repair.

→ Each of the cars _____.

UNIT 02 재귀대명사

⊘ Answer Key p.42

A GRAMMAR

빈칸에 알맞은 재귀대명사를 써서 문장을 완성하시오.

1 I kept some of the cookies for _____.

2 He accidentally hurt _____ while playing soccer.

3 The cat cleaned _____ after playing in the garden.

4 She can't turn on the light by _____. The switch is too high for her.

5 My brother and I should clean up the mess _____.

6 The children behaved _____ during the ceremony.

7 Mike, feel free to make _____ at home in the guest room.

8 Please help _____ to the food, everyone.

9 The car parked _____ by using advanced technology.

10 The girls enjoyed _____ at the concert last night.

B WRITING

우리말과 일치하도록 괄호 안의 말을 이용하여 문장을 완성하시오.

1 나는 거울을 자주 본다. (often, look at, in the mirror)

→ _____

2 그녀는 자신이 자랑스러울 거야. (must, be proud of)

→ _____

3 자기소개를 해 주시겠어요? (could, introduce)

→ _____

4 그는 읽고 쓰는 법을 스스로 익혔다. (teach, how to read and write)

→ _____

5 우리는 여행하는 동안 즐거운 시간을 보냈다. (enjoy, during the trip)

→ _____

UNIT 01 원급, 비교급, 최상급

☑ Answer Key p.43

A GRAMMAR 괄호 안의 말을 원급, 비교급, 최상급으로 바꿔 문장을 완성하시오.

1 The lake is as _____ as crystal. (clear)

2 The living room is _____ than the kitchen. (big)

3 This restaurant serves the _____ pizza in town. (good)

4 He is as _____ as a movie star. (handsome)

5 Jane is _____ than her brother. (careful)

6 The results are _____ than I expected. (bad)

7 This is the _____ question of the five. (easy)

8 The weather today is not as _____ as yesterday. (sunny)

9 Autumn is the _____ season of the year. (colorful)

10 She solved the puzzle _____ than anyone else. (quickly)

B WRITING 주어진 말을 바르게 배열하여 문장을 완성하시오. (필요시 형태를 바꿀 것)

1 a chef / good / as / cooks / as

→ My mother _____.

2 fast / of the three / the / is / runner

→ He _____.

3 than / light / the metal one / is

→ The plastic spoon _____.

4 interesting / as / is / as / I / not / expected

→ The book _____.

5 the / expensive / is / in the shop / item / little

→ It _____.

UNIT 02 여러 가지 비교 표현

⊘ Answer Key p.43

A GRAMMAR

괄호 안에서 알맞은 것을 고르시오.

1 I threw the ball as far as (could, possible).

2 My bike is (much, very) faster than yours.

3 I'm getting (many and many, more and more) tired.

4 Tolstoy is one of the (greater, greatest) writers in history.

5 He scored (higher, highest) than any other student in the class.

6 This shirt costs (two, twice) as much as that one.

7 It is the (worse, worst) storm I have ever experienced.

8 The higher you climb, the (colder, coldest) it gets.

9 The building is taller than any other (one, ones) in the city.

10 The *Mona Lisa* is one of the most famous (painting, paintings) in the world.

B WRITING

우리말과 일치하도록 괄호 안의 말을 이용하여 문장을 완성하시오.

1 풍선이 점점 더 커졌다. (big)

→ The balloon got _____.

2 나이가 들면 들수록 그는 더 현명해졌다. (old, wise)

→ _____ he got, _____ he became.

3 그 창고는 내 침실의 세 배만큼 넓다. (large)

→ The warehouse is _____ my bedroom.

4 바퀴는 역사상 가장 위대한 발명품들 중의 하나이다. (great, invention)

→ The wheel is _____ in history.

5 금성은 태양계에서 다른 어떤 행성보다 더 뜨겁다. (hot, planet)

→ Venus is _____ in our solar system.

UNIT 01 주격, 소유격 관계대명사

⊘ Answer Key p.43

A
GRAMMAR

다음 두 문장을 〈보기〉와 같이 한 문장으로 바꿔 쓰시오. (who, which, whose를 사용할 것)

> | 보기 | I met a man. He lives on the fifth floor.
> → I met a man who lives on the fifth floor.

1 He wants a house. It has two bedrooms.

→ _____

2 I know the man. He is standing at the door.

→ _____

3 Jessica has a dog. Its name is Happy.

→ _____

4 Bali is an island. It is located in Indonesia.

→ _____

B
WRITING

어법상 틀린 부분을 바르게 고쳐 문장을 다시 쓰시오.

1 The gift is for you that is on the table.

→ _____

2 The girl won the race received the trophy.

→ _____

3 I know a man who his son is a pianist.

→ _____

4 Look at the two dogs that is playing with the ball.

→ _____

5 Do you have a friend who live in a foreign country?

→ _____

⊘ Answer Key p.43

A

GRAMMAR

괄호 안에서 알맞은 것을 고르시오.

1 He is the man (whom, which) we all respect.

2 I don't like people (who, whom) never stop talking.

3 The movie (whom, which) we saw was very good.

4 Alex greeted his neighbor (whom, which) he often saw.

5 (Which, What) I want is more freedom.

6 Isaac saw a bird (which, whose) had a long beak.

7 The thing (that, what) you need is patience.

8 The present (that, what) I received was a photo frame.

9 I don't understand (that, what) you're talking about.

10 He talked about the book (that, what) he read recently.

B

WRITING

밑줄 친 부분을 바르게 고쳐 문장을 다시 쓰시오.

1 The museum <u>whom</u> we visited is on Park Avenue.

→ _____

2 The boys I met yesterday <u>was</u> my classmates.

→ _____

3 Can you describe the bag <u>you lost it</u>?

→ _____

4 I can't believe <u>that she did</u> last night.

→ _____

5 All <u>what he said</u> is certainly true.

→ _____

01 등위접속사, 상관접속사

⊘ Answer Key p.43

A

괄호 안에서 알맞은 것을 고르시오.

1 My little brother hates carrots (and, but) broccoli.

2 She can travel to Europe by plane (but, or) by train.

3 I love cats, (so, but) my mom doesn't like them.

4 It is raining hard, (or, so) we will stay inside.

5 Turn left, (and, or) you will see the public library.

6 Put on sunscreen, (and, or) you will get a sunburn.

7 The weather was neither too hot (or, nor) too cold.

8 Mr. Porter is not only smart (and, but) also funny.

9 Both the park (and, or) the beach are great places to go for a walk.

10 Either John or Mary (has, have) to prepare dinner tonight.

B

우리말과 일치하도록 괄호 안의 말을 이용하여 문장을 완성하시오.

1 그 타코는 맵지만 맛있다. (spicy, delicious)

→ The taco is _____.

2 네 방을 청소해, 그렇지 않으면 너는 네 용돈을 받지 못할 거야. (get, allowance)

→ Clean your room, _____.

3 그 젊은 남성 밴드는 한국에서뿐만 아니라 미국에서도 인기가 있다. (well, in Korea, in America)

→ The boy band is popular _____.

4 축구와 탁구 둘 다 내가 가장 좋아하는 운동이다. (both, football, table tennis)

→ _____ my favorite sports.

5 Andrew와 그의 친구들 모두 답을 알지 못한다. (nor, friend, know)

→ _____ the answer.

⊘ Answer Key p.44

A
GRAMMAR

괄호 안에서 알맞은 것을 고르시오.

1 Bob went for a walk (after, because) he took a nap.

2 (Though, When) the bell rings, students can leave the classroom.

3 I'll wait at the café until you (finish, will finish) your work.

4 The plants will die (if, unless) you water them properly.

5 (While, If) you give me your phone number, I will call you later.

6 (Because, Although) she was tired, she continued to study.

7 Mary can't walk to school (because, though) she lives far from it.

8 It was (so, such) hot that I drank a cold glass of water.

9 He was (so, such) a fast runner that he won the race easily.

10 I put on a raincoat (so, such) that I wouldn't get wet in the rain.

B
WRITING

우리말과 일치하도록 괄호 안의 말을 이용하여 문장을 완성하시오.

1 비가 그친다면 우리는 소풍을 갈 것이다. (it, stop raining)

→ We will go on a picnic _____.

2 그녀는 겁이 났지만 수영장에 뛰어들었다. (scared)

→ _____, she jumped into the pool.

3 그는 다이어트 중이기 때문에 후식을 먹는 것을 피한다. (on a diet)

→ _____, he avoids eating desserts.

4 John은 그의 아내가 저녁 식사를 준비하고 있는 동안 집을 청소했다. (wife, prepare dinner)

→ John cleaned the house _____.

5 그녀는 매우 훌륭한 요리사여서 모두가 그녀의 음식을 아주 좋아한다. (a good cook)

→ _____ that everyone loves her meals.

03 명사절 접속사 that, 간접의문문

⊘ Answer Key p.44

A
GRAMMAR

다음 두 문장을 〈보기〉와 같이 한 문장으로 바꿔 쓰시오.

> | 보기 | I don't know. + Where does she live?
> → I don't know where she lives.

1 Do you know? + What time is it?

→ _____

2 I asked her. + Who took my phone?

→ _____

3 I don't remember. + Where did I park my car?

→ _____

4 I'm not sure. + Does she prefer coffee or tea?

→ _____

B
WRITING

어법상 틀린 부분을 바르게 고쳐 문장을 다시 쓰시오.

1 It is amazing what she can speak five languages.

→ _____

2 The problem is we don't have enough money.

→ _____

3 He wants to know where is the post office.

→ _____

4 I wonder what does she like to do in her free time.

→ _____

5 If Jane will accept my invitation is uncertain.

→ _____

⊘ Answer Key p.44

A
GRAMMAR

〈보기〉와 같이 직설법 문장을 가정법 문장으로 바꿔 쓰시오.

> | 보기 | As she doesn't keep her promises, I don't trust her.
> → <u>If she kept her promises, I would trust her.</u>

1 As I am not feeling well, I won't join you for dinner.

→ _____

2 As he doesn't have enough money, he can't buy the bicycle.

→ _____

3 As it is so dark, we can't go for a walk.

→ _____

4 As traffic is so bad, we cannot get to the show on time.

→ _____

B
WRITING

밑줄 친 부분을 바르게 고쳐 문장을 다시 쓰시오.

1 <u>If she has more experience</u>, she would get the job.

→ _____, she would get the job.

2 <u>If you were not careful</u>, you may break the plate.

→ _____, you may break the plate.

3 <u>Kevin can give us some advice</u> if he were here.

→ _____ if he were here.

4 <u>You would get a stomachache</u> if you eat too much.

→ _____ if you eat too much.

5 <u>If I am you</u>, I would wear comfortable shoes for hiking.

→ _____, I would wear comfortable shoes for hiking.